EARTH
SONG

EARTH
SONG

INSIDE
**MICHAEL
JACKSON'S**
MAGNUM
OPUS

JOSEPH VOGEL

BlakeVision Books
New York

Library of Congress Cataloging-in-Publication Data
Vogel, Joseph, 1981-
Earth Song: Inside Michael Jackson's Magnum Opus/ Joseph
Vogel
p.   cm.

ISBN 13: 978-0981650678
ISBN 10: 0981650678
1. Jackson, Michael, 1958-2009—Criticism and Interpretation
2. Jackson, Michael, 1958-2009—Popular Music—United
States—History and Criticism
3. Vogel, Joseph. I. Title.

1 2 3 4 5 6 7 8 9 10

Printed in the United States of America

Dedicated to Sofi and Jude

They that walked in darkness sang songs in the olden days—Sorrow Songs—for they were weary at heart.
– W.E.B. DuBois, 1903

Now, more than ever, the world needs leaders who can inspire their fellow citizens with a fiery sense of mission, not a nationalistic or military campaign but a universal crusade to save the planet. Unless mankind embraces that cause totally, and without delay, it may have no alternative to the bang of nuclear holocaust or the whimper of slow extinction.
–*Time*, January 1989

A human being is part of the whole, called by us Universe, a part limited in time and space. He experiences himself, his thoughts and feelings as something separated from the rest—a kind of optical delusion of his consciousness. This delusion is a kind of prison for us, restricting us to our personal desires and to affection for a few persons nearest to us. Our task must be to free ourselves from this prison by widening our circle of compassion to embrace all living creatures and the whole of nature in its beauty.
– Albert Einstein, 1950

I know why the caged bird beats his wing
Till its blood is red on the cruel bars.
– Paul Laurence Dunbar, 1899

CONTENTS

EARTH SONG

In the Beginning

Michael Jackson was alone in his hotel room, pacing.

He was in the midst of the second leg of his *Bad World Tour*, an unprecedented, 123-date concert spectacular that stretched over nearly two years. The tour would become the largest-grossing and most-attended concert series in history.

Just days earlier, Jackson had performed in Rome at Flaminio Stadium to an ecstatic sold-out crowd of over 30,000 fans. In his downtime, he visited the Sistine Chapel and St. Peter's Cathedral at the Vatican with manager Frank Dileo, Quincy Jones and legendary composer, Leonard Bernstein. Later, they drove to Florence where Jackson stood alone beneath Michelangelo's masterful sculpture, *David*, gazing up in awe.[1]

Now he was in Vienna, Austria, music capital of the Western world. It was here that Mozart's brilliant *Symphony No. 25* and haunting *Requiem* were composed, that Beethoven studied under Haydn and played his first symphony. And it was here, at the Vienna Marriott on June 1, 1988 that Michael Jackson's magnum opus, "Earth Song," was born.

The six-and-a-half-minute piece that materialized over the next seven years was unlike anything heard before in popular music. Social anthems and protest songs had long been part of the heritage of rock—but not like this. "Earth Song" was something more epic, dramatic, and primal. Its roots were deeper; its vision more panoramic. It was a modern-day "sorrow song" haunted by voices of the past; a lamentation torn from the pages of the Old Testament; an apocalyptic prophecy in the tradition of Blake, Yeats and Eliot.

It conveyed musically what Picasso's masterful aesthetic protest, *Guernica*, conveyed in art.[2] Inside its swirling scenes of destruction and suffering were voices—crying, pleading, shouting to be heard (*"What about us?"*).

---

[1] This moment is documented on film. Jackson is dressed in black pants and a red shirt with his signature loafers and white socks. He walks toward the famous sculpture alone, in silhouette.

[2] Incidentally, Picasso's painting was similarly dismissed by critics as the childish vision of an eccentric. It is now widely considered one of the most important art works of the 20th century.

"Earth Song" would become the most successful environmental anthem ever recorded, topping the charts in over fifteen countries and eventually selling over seven million copies. Yet critics never quite knew what to make of it. Its unusual fusion of opera, rock, gospel, and blues sounded like nothing on the radio. It defied almost every expectation of a traditional anthem. In place of nationalism, it envisioned a world without division or hierarchy. In place of religious dogma or humanism, it yearned for a broader vision of ecological balance and harmony. In place of simplistic propaganda for a cause, it was a genuine artistic expression. In place of a jingly chorus that could be plastered on a T-shirt or billboard, it offered a wordless, universal cry.

Privilege and Pain

Jackson remembered the exact moment the melody came.

It was his second night in Vienna. Outside his hotel, beyond Ring Strasse Boulevard and the sprawling Stadtpark, he could see the majestically lit museums, cathedrals, and opera houses. It was a world of culture and privilege far removed from his boyhood home in Gary, Indiana. Jackson was staying in elegant conjoining suites lined with large windows and a breathtaking view. Yet for all the surrounding opulence, mentally and emotionally he was somewhere else.

It wasn't mere loneliness (though his prolonged isolation took its toll especially while on tour). It was something deeper—a pain that connected him to the pain of others, a pain indeed that he largely felt as he identified with the pain of others. As James Baldwin wrote: "You think your pain and your heartbreak are unprecedented in the history of the world, but then you read. It was books that taught me that the things that tormented me most were the very things that connected me with all the people who were alive, or who had ever been alive."[3] So it was with Jackson. He described his childhood and adolescence as a time of profound sadness and isolation. But books, music, film, paintings—*art*—had rescued him and bound him to a larger world of struggle, suffering, magic and beauty. It had given his life purpose.

When a work of art moved him, he obsessed over it. He would cross into its creative space and dwell inside its emotions, its characters, its textures and stories — sometimes for hours, sometimes for days. One such obsession at this time was with renowned artist Gottfried Helnwein's *Beautiful Victims*, a series of hyper-realistic watercolors and photographs from the 1970 and 80s that depict children in states of anguish and solitude. Helnwein's work is rooted in German expressionism. His subjects are often bandaged and presented against stark backdrops, highlighting their wounded and alienated condition.[4]

Jackson eventually used two of these pieces in

---

[3] *James Baldwin: Collected Essays.* Ed. by Toni Morrison. Library of America, 1998.

[4] "My work is not an answer," says Helnwein. "It is a question."

modified form for his *HIStory* booklet in 1995.[5] The photograph, "Lichtkind" (Child of Light), also served as inspiration for his song "Little Susie," which tells the macabre tale of a young girl who mysteriously dies after a life of neglect and abuse ("Lift her with care," he sings. "Oh, the blood in her hair").[6]

Jackson carried these images with him throughout his tour in 1988 until that July in Germany when he had the opportunity to meet the artist who created them. Jackson always felt a deep kinship with fellow artists—particularly those who somehow captured life the way he felt it. Gottfried Helnwein was surprised by how much Jackson knew about his work. He remembers him asking very specific questions about his techniques and inspirations. Helnwein came away convinced that this was no mere superficial pop star. "Not only do I think that he is highly intelligent but also outstandingly educated."[7] Helnwein did a brief photo shoot during his visit with Jackson in which he focused on the

---

[5] *HIStory: Past, Present and Future* CD Cover Booklet. Sony Music, 1995. p. 33: "Scream"- ("Das Lied/ The Song" watercolor, 1980); p. 37: "Little Susie"- ("Lichtkind/ Child of Light" photograph, grattage, 1972).

[6] Jackson shrugged off the criticism of such songs. "I don't care if people laugh or what they say. [Children] don't have a mouth to society…They need the world's awareness."

[7] "Beautiful Victim." Seven Bowie. MJJ-777.com. January 31, 2010.

singer's face with little lighting or makeup.[8] It was intended to capture the human being, not the icon, stripped down to his essence.

After their meeting, Jackson left a simple note to Helnwein that read:

Love to Gottfried Thanx for the magic

Michael Jackson[9]

---

[8] A portrait from this session now hangs in the Albertina Museum in Vienna, Austria. "He is extremely beautiful, fragile and totally unearthly," says Helnwein. "I always had the feeling that he is not standing on the floor but slightly floating on air. Michael Jackson knows that he appears like that on others and he also knows how to employ it."

[9] "Michael Jackson Meets With Helnwein in Germany."
http://www.helnwein-music.com/article596.html

We Are the World

Perhaps the most common trait associated with celebrity is narcissism. In 1988, Jackson certainly would have had reason to be self-absorbed. He was the most famous person on the planet. Everywhere he travelled, he created mass hysteria. The day after his sold-out concert at Prater Stadium in Vienna, an AP article ran, "130 Fans Faint at Jackson Concert."[10] If the Beatles were more popular than Jesus, as John Lennon once claimed, Jackson had the entire Holy Trinity beat.

Yet while Jackson enjoyed the attention—indeed,

---

[10] "130 Fans Faint at Jackson Concert." *Associated Press*. June 4, 1988.

even thrived on it in certain ways[11]—he also felt a profound responsibility to use his celebrity for more than fame and fortune. In 2000, *The Guinness Book of World Records* cited him as the most philanthropic pop star in history.[12] "When you have seen the things I have seen and travelled all over the world, you would not be honest to yourself and the world to [look away]," Jackson explained.[13]

At nearly every stop on his *Bad World Tour*, he visited orphanages and hospitals. Just days before arriving in Vienna, while in Rome, he stopped by the Bambin Gesu Children's

---

[11] This, after all, was the same artist who had his managers read P.T. Barnum's autobiography and proclaimed that he wanted his "whole life to be the greatest show on earth."

[12] Over his lifetime Jackson gave more than $300 million dollars and countless hours of his time to various charities and non-profits, including AIDS Project L.A., American Cancer Society, AmeriCares, Big Brothers/Big Sisters, Brotherhood Crusade, Brothman Burn Center, Camp Ronald McDonald, Childhelp U.S.A., Children's Institute International, Cities and Schools Scholarship Fund, Congressional Black Caucus, Dakar Foundation, Dreamstreet Kids, Dreams Come True Charity, Elizabeth Taylor AIDS Foundation, I Have a Dream Foundation, Juvenile Diabetes Foundation, Make-A-Wish Foundation, Minority AIDS Project, NAACP, National Rainbow Coalition, Red Cross, Nelson Mandela Children's Fund, Partnership For a Drug-free California, Starlight Foundation, The Carter Center, The Sickle Cell Research Foundation, Transafrica, United Negro College Fund, UNESCO, UNICEF, Volunteers of America, and the YMCA, among others.

[13] *The Michael Jackson Tapes.* Shmuley Boteach. Vanguard Press, 2009.

Hospital, handing out gifts, taking pictures, and signing autographs. Before leaving, he pledged a donation of over $100,000 dollars.

Before and after concerts, Jackson had under-privileged and sick children brought backstage. "Every night the kids would come in on stretchers, so sick they could hardly hold their heads up," recalls voice coach Seth Riggs. "Michael would kneel down at the stretchers and put his face right down beside theirs so that he could have his picture taken with them, and then give them a copy to remember the moment. I couldn't handle it. I'd be in the bathroom crying. The kids would perk right up in his presence. If it gave them a couple days' more energy, to Michael it was worth it."[14]

A few years earlier, in 1985, Jackson was at the forefront of the U.S.A. for Africa effort, which helped provide both short and long-term relief in the wake of the largest famine ever to hit Ethiopia (over one million people died and several million more were left destitute following a severe regional drought in 1984). The Jackson-Lionel Richie-penned anthem, "We are the World," not only became the fastest selling single in history (and the bestselling single of the 1980s), it helped bring in proceeds of over $50 million dollars. These funds were used to send over 120 tons of supplies, including high-protein biscuits, water, medicine,

---

[14] *Michael Jackson: The Magic and the Madness.* J. Randy Taraborrelli. Pan Books, 2004.

tents and clothing. Later funds were also used for over seventy recovery and development projects.[15]

Jackson was proud of what the song accomplished. The idea that thousands of malnourished children were fed because of a simple song thrilled and inspired him. It showed him in a very concrete way the power of music to bring people together, to raise awareness and action, to heal the world.[16]

Yet in the years that followed, he also realized it wasn't enough.[17] "We Are the World" didn't end hunger or poverty; it didn't solve the complicated socio-political issues,

---

[15] "We Are the World Passes Goal." Jeff Wilson. Associated Press. October 9, 1986.

[16] In 1991, Jackson released "Heal the World," which he described as a "public awareness song" intended to raise money and consciousness for humanitarian issues around the world. The following year, he officially launched the Heal the World Foundation. It was designed to be much more comprehensive than U.S.A. for Africa, addressing poverty, education, disease (including AIDS), and relief in the wake of wars, genocide and natural disasters. The foundation was quite active in its first few years, dedicating funds and resources to inner-city youth, children's hospitals and war refugees. While the intentions were noble, however, Jackson never had the time or skillset necessary to sustain such a complicated operation over the long haul and the Foundation was reportedly disbanded in 2002.

[17] In a 1988 interview with *Ebony/Jet*, Jackson was asked: "When you look in the mirror, are you happy with what you see?

"In what way?" he responded.

"Just when you look – in terms of that social philosophy?"

"I'm never totally satisfied," he said. "I always wish the world could be a better place. No, not at all."

power dynamics and institutional corruption that were largely to blame for the severity of the African famine. Critics were quick to point out these shortcomings, often deriding Jackson as "self-indulgent" and "naïve" for trying. Songs like "We Are the World" and "Man in the Mirror" were dismissed as simplistic, utopian childishness (music critic Greil Marcus wrote off the former song as nothing more than a Pepsi jingle, while the *New York Times'* Jon Pareles wrote off the latter as "activism for hermits"). Jackson's social vision offered global idealism, triumph and easy resolution, they argued, while the material conditions of the real world only worsened.

It was a critique that haunted Jackson while he toured. He believed the critics had it wrong; he believed they couldn't *feel* what the music meant to people—what it meant to *him*. It wasn't about political prescriptions; it was about awakening, connecting, healing. Change, he believed, began within individual hearts and minds.

Yet even he wondered at times: In the face of such relentless suffering and tragedy, what could an artist realistically hope to change? What could a song actually achieve?

I Feel Them Inside Me

Whike performing or helping children in face-to-face situations, Jackson could push away his feelings of inadequacy, doubt and despair. When crowds all over the world swayed and sang along to "Man in the Mirror"—when he could *experience* some small sliver of the world made harmonious—he was happy. He was in his element. But when he returned to his hotel room, the pain and confusion often returned.[18] "The contrast between the King of Pop on stage and the same person in private situations was enormous," remembers acclaimed Belgian composer François Glorieux,

---

[18] "Any great artist is wrestling with their sadness and loneliness, their fears, anxieties and insecurities," observes Cornell West, "and they're transfiguring those into complicated forms of expression that affect our hearts, minds and souls and remind us of who we are as human beings, the fragility of our human status and the inevitability of death…[Michael] was able to express himself in such a way that he allowed us to have a sense of what it feels like to be alive." "Georgetown professor assesses Michael Jackson's cultural legacy." *The Tavis Smiley Show*. PBS. June 30, 2009.

who first met Jackson in 1987 and went on to classically arrange several of Jackson's songs. "The press described him as an untouchable and impossible man. But I discovered a completely different guy: extremely sensitive, emotional and even shy…The first hour I met him he asked me to describe my childhood. He didn't interrupt me once and listened to the whole story of my youth when bombs destroyed my home and killed three members of my family."[19] Glorieux met with Jackson on two other occasions, in 1989 and 1990. He describes these meetings as "the most emotional of my musical career. It was fantastic to discover so many common points of view: passion for music (without limits); for peace and freedom; love for animals and nature; and last but not least, [a concern for] humanity."[20]

Physician and author Deepak Chopra had a similar impression of the elusive pop star. "When we first met, around 1988," he recalls, "I was struck by the combination of charisma and woundedness that surrounded Michael. He would be swarmed by crowds at an airport, perform an exhausting show for three hours, and then sit backstage afterward, as we did one night in Bucharest, drinking bottled water, glancing over some Sufi poetry as I walked into the

---

[19] "François Glorieux: 'Do you know that he danced with me in his studio.'" Qtd. by Seven Bowie. MJJ-777.com. August 12, 2011. Also FrançoisGlorieux.com.
[20] *Ibid.*

room, and wanting to meditate."[21]

People sensed this sensitivity in Jackson from a very young age. It was one of the qualities that made him such a compelling performer, even as a child. For all the joy and vitality he exuded, there was always a certain sadness, a world-weary melancholy.

In his teens, Jackson began to develop the early seeds of his social vision and humanitarian ambition. "Politics can't save the world, so the music people should at least try," he said in a 1979 interview with *Blues & Soul.* "I could never just make records for people to buy and just get rich from. That's no good to me. There has to be more than that."[22]

Themes of brotherly love, acceptance, and social transformation populate his earliest self-written work, including "Can You Feel It," "There Must Be More to Life Than This," and "Be Not Always."

Over the ensuing decade, however, Jackson grew and evolved, both artistically and intellectually. His education was largely self-guided, but he approached it with an insatiable curiosity. Everywhere he toured he studied the culture and the people; he visited museums, galleries and bookstores as well as hospitals and orphanages. At his Neverland home he amassed

---

[21] "A Tribute to My Friend." Deepak Chopra. *The Huffington Post.* June 26, 2009.
[22] "Michael Jackson's Peacock Music." Tamika Jones and John Abbey. *Blues & Soul.* August 28, 1979.

a library of thousands of books, videos and tapes. He read widely, reached out to experts, and pursed issues that interested him passionately. Even his aversion to traditional politics dissipated somewhat by the late 1980s. While he was never a policy wonk, he began to see some of the motives, interests and forces that led to such widespread injustice, destruction and suffering.

1988 proved to be a critical turning point in his concern for the welfare of the planet. The news that year read like passages from scripture: there were heat waves and droughts, massive wildfires and earthquakes, genocides and famine. Violence escalated in the Holy Land, as forests were ravaged in the Amazon, and garbage, oil and sewage swept up on shores. In place of *Time's* Person of the Year, 1988's year-end cover story was dedicated to the "endangered earth."[23] It suddenly occurred to many people that we were literally destroying our own home.

Jackson was particularly concerned about the rapid deforestation of the Amazon. The Amazon Rainforest contains more than half of the planet's remaining rainforest land and is the most species-rich territory in the world. An estimated one-

---

[23] From *Time*: "No single individual, no event, no movement captured imaginations or dominated headlines more than the clump of rock and soil and water and air that is our common home." "Planet of the Year: What on Earth Are We Doing." *Time*. January 2, 1989.

third of the planet's biodiversity is in the Amazon and one-fifth of its freshwater. Scientists estimate that the Amazon has between 85 billion and 100 billion tons of carbon stored in its trees and shrubs, which equates to about 11 years' worth of global emissions. It is also home to many indigenous communities whose way of life has frequently been threatened by deforestation.

In 1988 and 1989, international attention to the Amazon reached its height when projects such as the construction of a transoceanic highway, dams, and further clearing for large soybean ranchers threatened to destroy unprecedented amounts of rainforest. Several high-profile celebrities became involved, including actor Marlon Brando, Latin American author Gabriel García Márquez, and recording artist Sting.[24] Saving the rainforests became a rallying call for the socially conscious in the late 1980s. It was both an environmental issue and a human rights issue. Remarkably, the heightened public awareness and the

---

[24] Beginning in late 1988, Sting teamed up with Chief Raoni (whose Kayapo people resided in the plain lands of the Mato Grosso and Pará in Brazil), embarking on a seventeen-country campaign to draw attention to the Amazon's plight. In 1989, he founded the Rainforest Foundation with his wife Trudie Styler, whose mission was to "to protect and support indigenous peoples and traditional forest populations in their efforts to protect their environment and fulfill their right to a secure, healthy and ecologically sound environment." Since 1989, it has helped protect over 28 million acres of forest and won several legal battles upholding the rights of indigenous peoples. It currently operates in over twenty countries.

collective efforts of many groups and individuals had a
meaningful impact. By 1991, deforestation slowed to one of
the lowest rates on record. By 1993, the unification of the
Xingu indigenous lands gave birth to one of the most
important rainforest reserves in the world (an estimated 6.7
million acres).[25]

The Amazon Rainforest, of course, was just one of
many issues. 1989 was also the year of the infamous Exxon
Valdez oil spill in Alaska, considered one of the most
devastating human-caused environmental disasters in history.
Months later the student-led protests at Tiananmen Square in
China resulted in tragedy as over one thousand innocent
civilians were massacred by troops with assault rifles and
tanks.

Some people grow accustomed to reading or watching
the news casually, passively. They become numb to the
horrifying images and stories projected on the screen. Yet such
stories frequently moved Jackson to tears. He internalized
them and often felt physical pain in response. When people
scoffed at his sensitivity or told him to simply enjoy his own
good fortune, he got angry. He believed in the poet John

---

[25] Unfortunately, by 1995—the year "Earth Song" was released—
many people had lost interest and deforestation rates spiked higher
than ever. Recent efforts to draw attention back to the Amazon
Rainforest, and rainforests throughout the world, have made
connections to climate change and shown their importance to
sustainability.

Donne's dictum that "no man is an island." For Jackson, however, the idea extended to life in all forms: nature, animals, and people across countries, cultures and races—the whole planet was connected and intrinsically valuable.

"[For the average person]," he explained, "he sees problems 'out there' to be solved. Maybe they will be, maybe they won't...But I don't feel that way—those problems aren't 'out there,' really. I feel them inside me. A child crying in Ethiopia, a seagull struggling pathetically in an oil spill...a teenage soldier trembling with terror when he hears the planes fly over: Aren't these happening in me when I see and hear about them?"[26] One time, during a dance rehearsal, Jackson had to stop because an image he saw earlier that day of a dolphin trapped in a net made him so emotionally distraught. "From the way its body was tangled in the lines," he explained, "you could read so much agony."[27]

When Jackson performed, he could feel these turbulent emotions surging through him. With his dancing and singing, he tried to transfuse the suffering—give it expression and meaning. It was liberating. For a brief moment, he could take his audience (and himself) to an alternative world of harmony and ecstasy. "There is no greater bliss," Jackson explained. "[You] become one with the music,

---

[26] *Dancing the Dream: Poems and Reflections.* Michael Jackson. Doubleday, 1992.
[27] *Ibid.*

one with the audience...You start to play off each other and start to know where you are going before you get there...You feel you are transformed."[28]

But inevitably, he had to come back down. The music would stop, the lights would dim, the crowd would file out. And he would be whisked away by his entourage to another hotel in another city.

---

[28] *The Michael Jackson Tapes.* Shmuley Boteach. Vanguard Press, 2009.

This is Her Song

As was customary during the *Bad World Tour*, Jackson was "smuggled" into his Vienna hotel through the back staff entrance along with Bill Bray, his longtime security chief, and other members of his entourage.

Once inside, he typically showered off and read a book; sometimes he would sketch in his art pad or watch a movie. On the night after his concert at Prater Stadium thousands of fans converged outside the hotel, chanting his name. Jackson finally emerged in one of the windows, wearing a grey and blue pinstriped pajama top and red flannel pants. He waved below to the euphoric crowd before running back to the bathroom, signing some promotional photos and tossing them out the window.[29]

For however long his stay was in a given city, his hotel

---

[29] I was alerted to the existence of this footage by Michael Jackson researcher Chris Merante.

room became both sanctuary and prison cell. The maids at the Vienna Marriott Hotel remember him being extremely private. When they came into clean or bring food, he "disappear[ed] into another room."[30] He was the biggest star in the world, but wanted nothing more, at times like these, than the anonymity of a normal person.

It was during this brief stay in Vienna, however, that inspiration struck. "It just suddenly dropped into my lap," he recalled of the moment.[31]   Earth's song. A song from her perspective, her voice. A lamentation and a plea.

The chorus came to him first—a wordless cry. He grabbed his tape player and pressed record. *Aaaaaaaaah Oooooooooh.*

The chords were simple, but beautiful: A-flat minor to C-sharp triad; A-flat minor seventh to C-sharp triad; then

---

[30] "Wohnen Wie der King of Pop." Wiener Bezirkszeitung Nr. 25, 23. Juni 2010. Translated by Manu Wedam.

[31] Jackson's full quote about how "Earth Song" first came to him: "I remember writing 'Earth Song' when I was in Austria, in a hotel, and I was feeling so much pain and so much suffering for the plight of the planet Earth. For me, this is Earth's Song, because I think nature is trying so hard to compensate for man's mismanagement of the Earth. And with the ecological imbalance going on, and a lot of the problems in the environment, I think Earth feels the pain, and she has wounds, and it's about some of the joys of the planet as well. But this is my chance to pretty much let people hear the voice of the planet. And this is 'Earth Song.' And that's what inspired it. And it just suddenly dropped into my lap when I was on tour in Austria."

modulating up, B-flat minor to E-flat triad. *That's it!* Jackson thought. He then worked out the introduction and some of the verses. He imagined its scope in his head. Nobody could see what he saw yet. But they would.

This, he felt, would be the most important song he'd ever composed.

Right Now Is the Moment of Eternity

Almost exactly one year later, when Jackson returned from touring, "Earth Song" (which was then referred to as "Earth" or "Planet Earth") was one of the first songs he brought in to work on.

It was the summer of 1989. He had recently purchased his Neverland Ranch in the Santa Ynez Valley and felt a renewed sense of purpose and vision for his work. "Michael was inspired by touring and seeing the world," said recording engineer, Matt Forger. "He came back with certain impressions. His social commentary kicked up a notch or two. Most of the early songs we worked on—"Black or White," "They Don't Care About Us," "Heal the World," and "Earth

Song"—were more socially conscious. His consciousness of the planet was much more in the forefront."[32]

Jackson's spiritual worldview had also transformed. Raised a Jehovah's Witness, he was taught to believe in a God that was rigid and demanding (including the commandment not to celebrate holidays or birthdays). The main purpose of life was to prepare oneself and others for Armageddon, which Witnesses believed was imminent and futile to try to delay or prevent. The goal, rather, was to become one of the elite righteous members (the 144,000) that would survive and preside over the earth once it was cleansed of wickedness. (If one didn't make the top tier, they could still be part of a second class of Witnesses who were allowed to live in paradise).[33]

For much of his life, Jackson tried to believe these doctrines. He pored over the Bible and felt deep anxiety about his eternal salvation. He frequently asked questions of church elders about doctrines he found confusing or unfair. Yet by 1987, he had learned and experienced enough to decide to officially resign from the faith. In a poem, Jackson wrote, "But I have chosen to break and be free/ Cut those ties, so I can see/ Those bonds that imprisoned me in memories of pain/ Those

---

[32] Author Interview with Matt Forger. May 15, 2011.

[33] "Jehovah's Witness." *The Columbia Encyclopedia.* Columbia University Press. 2011. Also see *Apocalypse Delayed: The Story of Jehovah's Witnesses.* James Penton. University of Toronto Press, 1997.

judgments, interpretations that cluttered my brain."[34]

In its place, he developed a much more inclusive, liberating understanding of himself, the world and the divine (informed, in part, by his exposure to Eastern and Transcendentalist ideas). "It's strange that God doesn't mind expressing Himself/ Herself in all the religions of the world, while people still cling to the notion that their way is the only right way," he wrote in his 1992 book, *Dancing the Dream.*[35] In another piece, in place of his prior conception of the afterlife, he writes: "Heaven is here/ Right now is the moment of eternity/ Don't fool yourself/ Reclaim your bliss."[36]

This new understanding had a profound impact on his creativity, including "Earth Song." If God wasn't a demanding father, but an inspiring presence or energy like music and nature—if the global destruction of Armageddon wasn't inevitable, as he was taught, but something to try to pre-emptively heal—this had crucial implications for his artistic and social vision. It gave a new urgency to his work. It also helped push his social commentary into more direct, challenging territory. "Earth Song" wasn't about faith or triumph; it was about pain and indignation.

Jackson, of course, was still informed by his religious

---

[34] *Dancing the Dream: Poems and Reflections.* Michael Jackson. Doubleday, 1992.
[35] *Ibid.*
[36] *Ibid.*

upbringing. "Earth Song" is rooted in the fervent jeremiads and apocalyptic passion of the Bible—but it was now liberated from one particular creed and fused with more social aims. Jackson wasn't content to simply wait for God to fix the world or placated by promises of paradise. "It starts with us," he insisted. "It's *us*! Or it will never be done."[37]

---

[37] Michael Jackson's *This Is It*. Directed by Kenny Ortega. DVD. Sony Pictures, 2009.

Let the Music Create Itself

B̲y the time Jackson returned to Westlake Studio in June of 1989, he was bursting with creative ideas. On a board by the mixing desk, he put up a quote by John Lennon: "When the real music comes to me," it read, "the music of the spheres, the music that surpasseth understanding—that has nothing to do with me, 'cause I'm just the channel. The only joy for me is for it to be given to me, and to transcribe it like a medium… Those moments are what I live for."[38] The words resonated deeply for Jackson: "channeling" was exactly how he viewed creativity.

"Let the music create itself," he often reminded

---

[38] Matt Forger mentioned the John Lennon quote in one of our interviews, but couldn't remember exactly what it said. I subsequently found it in the background of a photo taken in the studio. The full quote can be found in the book: *John Lennon: In His Own Words*. Ken Lawrence. Andrews McMeel Publishing, 2005.

himself. To Jackson, Lennon was a kindred soul: a similarly eccentric talent with the ambition, idealism, and defiance to re-imagine the world.

Still, Jackson knew it took time and effort to achieve what he saw and heard in his head. Some songs could be completed within weeks, while others took months, even years. He sometimes compared the creative process to an artist chipping away at a sculpture. "[You're] just freeing it. It's already in there. It's already there."[39]

With "Earth Song," he had the basic concept and melody worked out, but he wasn't quite sure yet how to execute it. Like a director, he needed the right creative team to help realize his vision.

---

[39] Interview with Regina Jones. *Vibe*. March 2002.

An Epic in Embryo

In late July 1989, Jackson called up Bill Bottrell (whom he called "Billy"), a young, smart, up-and-coming engineer and producer Jackson had worked with at his Hayvenhurst studio during the *Victory* and *Bad* sessions. While none of their collaborations made the *Bad* album, the pair developed a strong creative chemistry that would result in some of the *Dangerous* album's best tracks (including "Black or White" and "Give In To Me") and several other quality outtakes (including "Streetwalker" and "Monkey Business").

Bad was Jackson's last album with music legend Quincy Jones. The decision not to renew with Jones caused some frayed feelings, but Jackson felt the move was necessary for his artistic growth. The *Dangerous* album was his first chance to act as executive producer, and he was thrilled to finally be in complete creative control.

Bottrell was a surprisingly natural fit for "Earth

Song." Prior to working with Jackson, his musical résumé was eclectic. After being hired for an ELO project by renowned producer Jeff Lynne (who had also worked with the likes of Bob Dylan, George Harrison, Tom Petty and Brian Wilson), Bottrell did freelance work as an engineer around Los Angeles. He was introduced to the Jacksons by John McClain, a talented executive in the urban music division at A&M Records who helped launch Janet Jackson's career in the mid-1980s.[40]

Bottrell's musical roots were in blues, folk and country, but he could adapt to just about any style, from prog rock, to New Wave, to synth pop. In addition to his work behind the desk, he also played multiple instruments, including guitar, piano, drums and harmonica. By 1990 he had gone from obscure freelance engineer to the pinnacle of the pop music industry, working with icons like Jackson and Madonna. The success and commercial aspects of the industry, however, were uncomfortable for Bottrell. He loved music for the sake of music, not to satisfy corporate executives. Soon after his work on *Dangerous*, he fled the Los Angeles scene and built his own studio called Toad Hall in Pasadena. Here, he began working with "marginalized artists," emphasizing the qualities he valued in music: authenticity,

---

[40] In 2009, following Jackson's death, John McClain was named co-executor of the Michael Jackson Estate along with Jackson's longtime attorney John Branca.

spontaneity, and the rawness and immediacy of a live performance. Bottrell went on to produce the debut albums of Sheryl Crow and Shelby Lynne, both of which won Grammy Awards.

Jackson was drawn to Bottrell's alternative sensibility, especially after a lifetime of working in the Motown ethos (and then with Quincy Jones). It allowed him the freedom to experiment in different styles and with different themes. Bottrell believed artists should tap into their musical roots, whatever those roots were. He created a loose environment in the studio, allowing Jackson to operate without the looming pressure of expectations. "The main thing that I do as a producer, for better or for worse," Bottrell says, "is to orchestrate emotions in a room toward something...To get a good performance, you need to set a mood — a vibe — and this has to do with the people and the environment, the room they're in...I don't overly plan things. I like it loose, and I like it somewhat chaotic."[41]

Most important to Jackson was the way he and Bottrell worked together and understood each other. "Michael was always prepared to listen and put his trust in me, but he was also a sort of guide all the time," recalls Bottrell, "He knew why I was there and, among all the songs he was

---

[41] "Pushing the Right Buttons." Paul Tingen. *Electronic Musician.* http://www.emusician.com/artists/0767/pushing-the-right-buttons/147203. July 1, 2007.

recording, what he needed from me...He has precise musical instincts. He has an entire record in his head and he tries to make people deliver it to him. Sometimes those people surprise him and augment what he hears, but really his job is to extract from musicians and producers and engineers what he hears when he wakes up in the morning."[42]

Like Matt Forger and others, Bill Bottrell sensed an intensification in Jackson's passion about social and ecological issues. It was a passion they shared.[43] They watched numerous documentaries together and discussed issues like deforestation, animal rights, and corporate imperialism. One day, Jackson brought in a VHS of the 1985 film *The Emerald Forest*, directed by John Boorman, which recounts the story of a Brazilian tribe (the "Invisible People") and rain forest under siege by corporate colonizers.[44] It is a familiar theme now,[45] but at the time of its release the movie was quite revolutionary, drawing public attention to the rapid destruction of the Amazon. Jackson loved the film and instructed Bottrell to watch and internalize it to "prepare" him

---

[42] "Classic Tracks: Michael Jackson's 'Black or White.'" *Sound on Sound*. Richard Buskin. August 2004.

[43] Bottrell became somewhat notorious in the music industry for his countercultural, anti-corporate, principled positions. This sensibility, however, was part of what made his role in "Earth Song" so important.

[44] Author Interview with Bill Bottrell. May 14, 2011.

[45] See films like *FernGully: The Last Rainforest* (1992) and James Cameron's blockbuster *Avatar* (2009).

to work on "Earth Song."[46]

When they arrived in the studio, Jackson let Bottrell listen to what he had: an intro (which Bottrell quickly put down on a grand piano), some verses, the chorus, and some rough lyrics. Bottrell was immediately taken by the two melody lines. He could hear the song had great potential.

Brad Buxer, a classically trained keyboardist who had worked with Stevie Wonder and was brought on board by Bottrell that summer, was equally impressed. "The chorus is beautiful," he said. "I love stuff like that—triads to minor 7 chords. One of the most magical aspects of music is when you mix things up. A lot of basic rock and roll is triads, and jazz is complex chords. No jazz musician would say 'Earth Song' is tricky, but it's not about being complex. If it's done right, it's gorgeous. It's like poetry. Subtlety is everything. Michael had a beautiful sense of art."[47]

---

[46] Author Interview with Bill Bottrell. May 14, 2011.
[47] Author Interview with Brad Buxer. May 16, 2011.

Earth Trilogy

Gradually, in the ensuing months the various parts of the song began to take shape. "It became quite the obsession for both of us," recalled Bottrell.[48]

Jackson's early concern was getting its size and tone right. He wanted it to have the passion and soul of a gospel song, the momentum of rock, and the linear arc of an opera. He wanted a sonic landscape that borrowed from ambient and world music, yet still managed to be classical and accessible. He didn't want it to be too complex or abstract since the song was intended to move masses of people. The key, then, was to make it "feel simple," but layer it with detail, texture, nuance,

---

[48] Author Interview with Bill Bottrell. May 27, 2011.

and richness.[49]

Jackson originally conceived of "Earth Song" as a trilogy (similar to "Will You Be There"), comprised of a modern orchestral piece, the main song, and a spoken poem (later released by itself as "Planet Earth"). In total, it would have been approximately thirteen minutes long. The poem, a couplet with thematic echoes of Wordsworth, Keats, and Whitman, among others, was essentially a cosmic love song to the planet. "In my veins, I've felt the mystery," Jackson wrote.

> Of corridors of time, books of history
> Life songs of ages, throbbing in my blood
> Have danced the rhythm of the tide and flood
> Your misty clouds, your electric storm
> Were turbulent tempests in my own form
> I've licked the salt, the bitter, the sweet
> Of every encounter, of passion, of heat
> Your riotous color, your fragrance, your taste
> Have thrilled my senses beyond all haste
> In your beauty I've known the how
> Of timeless bliss, this moment of now.[50]

---

[49] "With Michael," explains Matt Forger, "the foundation may be deceptively simple, but so much is happening. So much detail and work. He understood contrast. He was very particular about texture. He wanted ['Earth Song'] to feel fresh and new and have this kind of epic weight and momentum." Author Interview with Matt Forger. May 15, 2011.

Jackson's sensuous language evokes a different kind of relationship with the natural world: one of intimacy, wonder, and respect. It rejects the traditional Western notion that humans "own" nature and can do with it as they please.

For Jackson, nature was a source of profound joy, inspiration, and rejuvenation.[51] "The whole world abounds in magic," he wrote in a piece in his 1992 book, *Dancing the Dream*. "[Nature] has exposed the real illusion, our inability to be amazed by her wonders. Every time the sun rises, Nature is repeating one command, 'Behold!' Her magic is infinitely lavish, and all we have to do is appreciate it."[52]

Jackson worked with Jorge del Barrio on the orchestral introduction. An accomplished composer and

---

[50] *Dancing the Dream: Poems and Reflections.* Michael Jackson. Doubleday, 1992.

[51] Jackson was reading Emerson around this time. "In the woods, is perpetual youth," Emerson writes in his 1836 essay, "Nature," "a perennial festival...Standing on the bare ground, — my head bathed by the blithe air, and uplifted into infinite space, — all mean egotism vanishes. I become a transparent eye-ball; I am nothing; I see all; the currents of the Universal Being circulate through me; I am part or particle of God." When Jackson came across this essay he was exhilarated. It is one of the reasons he bought Neverland Ranch, far away from the congestion and stress of the city. *Dancing the Dream* is filled with such Emersonian reflections about becoming transfused in nature.

[52] *Dancing the Dream: Poems and Reflections.* Michael Jackson. Doubleday, 1992.

conductor, del Barrio (who would later work with Jackson on several other songs, including "Who Is It" and "Morphine"), described working with Michael as "one of the most memorable experiences in [his] life." "He was so passionate about his music," he recalls. "We spent most of our time alone, creating. We were very much friends and creative forces together."[53] Jackson felt del Barrio was a perfect fit for what he hoped to accomplish with "Earth Song."

In contrast to the section of Beethoven's Ninth Symphony Jackson used to lead into "Will You Be There," the prelude to "Earth Song" was more ambient and primordial. It contained nature sounds, indigenous drums, deep synth pads, and lush strings. "I worked with Michael on creating an ominous sound," says del Barrio, "the beginning of the Earth as it might have sounded when it was created and life began and as it progressed into Mother Earth and eventually moved into 'Earth Song,' which tells of the demise of the planet in the hands of Man. Michael felt that this song was to be the one that ultimately would help save the world."[54]

---

[53] Author Inteview with Jorge del Barrio. Translated by Ramon del Barrio. June 15, 2011. "Michael thought my father was extraordinary and they also spent a lot time laughing and making jokes," says Ramon del Barrio, after speaking to his father. "Dad and Michael worked together for many years and I am sure there are so many songs that were not released as well."
[54] Author Inteview with Jorge del Barrio. Translated by Ramon del Barrio. June 15, 2011.

According to recording engineer, Matt Forger, it was "very modern, very avant-garde. He wanted to change the rules of a pop song, to stretch and experiment. It was a completely different sound for Michael. The whole concept was very ambitious."[55]

Ultimately, however, Jackson couldn't quite get the tripartite concept to work together the way he had hoped and decided to simply stick with the main part of the song. Still, many of the early ideas and sounds were implemented in del Barrio's orchestral arrangement for the song, including the dramatic strings.

Jackson also brought in Toto band members, Steve Porcaro and David Paich, to assist with synth programming. The atmosphere of the track, he knew, was crucial. The listener had to really *feel* it for it to effectively transport them. It also had to have a "beginning, a middle, and an end."[56] It had to tell a simple story that could be understood across cultures and languages. The challenge was accomplishing all of this in six and a half minutes.

---

[55] Author Interview with Matt Forger. May 15, 2011.
[56] While occasionally breaking his own rule, Jackson was a firm believer, in principle, in traditional forms of "storytelling."

Make it Big

Jackson was looking for something particularly unique and powerful for the bass. He came across a sound he really liked in the work of Guy Pratt, a renowned guitarist who was playing bass with Pink Floyd at the time. Pratt had also recently played on Madonna's hit, "Like a Prayer" (which Bottrell engineered).

Through Bottrell, Jackson extended the invitation to work on the track, and Pratt accepted. After learning of Jackson's vision for the song and hearing a demo, he laid down a massive, experimental octave-pedal bass line at Westlake Studio.[57] The deep, soul-vibrating sound heard on the record was achieved by using an octave divider, so that the

---

[57] In interviews and comedy routines Guy Pratt tells a much more elaborate story about his experience. Jackson, he says, was hiding behind the mixing desk giving instructions through a Samoan bodyguard. While it's a funny story, I am told by reliable sources present during these sessions that it didn't really happen.

bass was playing in two octaves at once. "That's what gave it that grandiosity," explained Bottrell.[58]

Jackson loved it. Indeed, the effect was impressive to the most discerning professionals. "'Earth Song' has a deeper bass than any track I've ever heard," said Brad Buxer. "It's remarkable. Usually you can mix a song down to two tracks on half-inch analog and get a little more punch in the bass, but when you mix to digital you can't because it will distort. That track somehow holds more of the bass elements, it's more saturated—so it gives the illusion of more low-end than a CD can actually hold. Billy and Bruce [Swedien] were masters at that. There's a magic in shaping those low frequencies, pulling certain elements out so you can get other elements in. Psychologically, it makes the bass sound as big and rich as possible."[59]

Soon after Pratt's session work, legendary British drummer Steve Ferrone (best known for his work with Tom Petty and Eric Clapton) came in to lay down the drum parts. Jackson and Bottrell communicated how epic it needed to be, especially after the second verse.[60] "It's this very heroic rock rhythm," says Bottrell. "And the drums just explode. Michael

---

[58] Author Interview with Bill Bottrell. May 14, 2011.

[59] Author Interview with Brad Buxer. May 17, 2011.

[60] During the *HIStory* sessions, Bruce Swedien added a TC Electronics M5000, highly modified, "Wooden Hall" reverb on the drums to further accentuate their power. *In the Studio With Michael Jackson*. Hal Leonard, 2009.

kept saying, 'Make it big, make it big.'"[61] Jackson initially wanted electronic drums for the track, but Ferrone convinced him to give real drums a chance. "I said, 'I'll do a deal with you," recalls Ferrone. "I'll cut it with electronic drums if you let me have a go at it on real drums.' And he said okay."[62]

Jackson listened to the electronic drum part first and loved it. He didn't feel another track was even necessary. It was perfect. But Ferrone reminded him of their deal. "Alright," Jackson agreed with a smile.

A while later he returned to Westlake Studio, and Steve Ferrone and Bill Bottrell let him hear the live drum version. Jackson was over the moon. "The real drums just move the air off those speakers," recalls Ferrone. "He went from just sitting there, listening, to dancing around the room. And that's what they used."[63]

Once most of the elements were in place, the legendary Andraé Crouch Choir (who previously sang on "Man in the Mirror" and participated on two other tracks on *Dangerous*) came in to sing their portion of the song's epic finale. The entire session was filmed (with multiple cameras) and reveals a remarkable scene of collaborative energy: Jackson

---

[61] Author Interview with Bill Bottrell. May 14, 2011.
[62] "British Drum Icon – Steve Ferrone." *British Drum Icons.* mikedolbear.com. http://www.mikedolbear.co.uk/story.asp?StoryID=1888.
[63] *Ibid.*

and Bottrell getting sounds in place and discussing the arrangement; rehearsals and final adjustments being made to the set up and equipment; the choir gathering in a circle and delivering its majestic chants.

"We gave them a tape to rehearse to a few days before with Michael's lead vocal," recalled Bottrell, "and they came in with the most wonderful arrangement."[64] The grand stereophonic sound was captured using two Neumann M-49 microphones and a vintage EMT 250 for reverb. The result was a powerful, dramatic climax with the natural energy of a live exchange.

---

[64] Author Interview with Bill Bottrell. May 14, 2011.

Discovering Everything You Can

Jackson and Bottrell continued to tinker with the track for over a year—the first several months at Westlake and later at Record One in Sherman Oaks, California. As the *Dangerous* sessions progressed, however, much of Jackson's attention shifted towards the rhythm tracks, particularly when new jack swing producer Teddy Riley was brought on board in early 1991. Still, Bottrell felt confident "Earth Song" would not only make the *Dangerous* album, but serve as its centerpiece.

As the album was wrapping up in the fall of 1991, Bottrell submitted the stem tape (a simple multi-track that embodies the mix). The song was now titled "What About Us" and Bottrell considered it "finished" besides some final vocal overdubs. "It was one of our priority tracks from the beginning," he said. "I was very proud of it."[65]

Yet to his (and many others') surprise, Jackson passed it up for the final track list of *Dangerous*. Bottrell was deeply disappointed. "I wasn't present when they had the Sony people out to listen to all of the stuff at the playback, so I found out later."[66]

Jackson understood Bottrell's disappointment. He was disappointed as well. The song meant a great deal to him. Yet his ultimate commitment was to the song—it had to be just right before he could release it, and he didn't feel it was quite there.

All who worked with Jackson understood that he was a painstaking perfectionist: every detail, from conception to production to mixing and mastering, had to be exactly what he wanted before he would "lock it in cement." It could be frustrating at times. Some collaborators worked with him for months, and none of the resulting material ended up on an album. Sometimes he admittedly over-thought or overworked a track, when he should have simply stuck with an early version.

Yet frequently the perfectionism paid off, as some new revelation would occur to him that would make the song stronger. "Michael has always felt better really fleshing out

---

[65] Author Interview with Bill Bottrell. May 27, 2011.
[66] Author Interview with Bill Bottrell. May 14, 2011.

something over a long period of time to discover everything that he can about it," acknowledged Bottrell. "There was a process that I learned well, that any MJ release went through: a process of vetting, re-thinking, replacing midi with live players, etc. It was a long process."[67] In many cases, the average listener probably wouldn't even notice the differences, but Jackson felt an intrinsic obligation to make his art "as perfect as humanly possible."

With "Earth Song," beyond the unfinished lyrics, his main concern was getting more momentum, energy, and power in the second half. While the falsetto cries (which Bottrell described as "very Marvin Gaye-ish") in the call and response were poignant, he wasn't sure it captured the outrage and urgency he wanted to convey. There were also some more minor nuances he wanted to tweak with the instrumentation and the mix. "Earth Song," then, would stay in the vaults for another four years as Jackson promoted and toured for *Dangerous*.

---

[67] "Michael Jackson's 'Black or White.'" Richard Buskin. *Sound on Sound*. August 2004. Also Gearslutz forum. "Post here if you worked on Michael Jackson's Dangerous album." June 27, 2009.

History in the Making

When recording began on *HIStory* in January of 1994 at The Hit Factory in New York, Jackson was excited to finally get back to work on "Earth Song." He felt confident it would find a home on the new record. The only questions were how to make it better and who to assist him in finalizing his vision.

As it turned out, Jackson was mostly satisfied with the demo he had worked out with Bottrell during the *Dangerous* sessions. The length, arrangement, and production remained almost exactly the same. Still, there were some crucial additions, most significantly in the climax of the song.

Jackson turned to renowned Canadian-born

"hitmaker" David Foster to help finish the track.[68] The winner of sixteen Grammy awards, Foster had worked with legends like Chicago, Barbara Streisand, Whitney Houston and Celine Dion (he had also worked briefly with Jackson in 1978 during the *Off the Wall* sessions).[69] His specialty was the power ballad, though his work in this genre also gave him a reputation for affectation and hyper-glossy production. In 1985, *Rolling Stone* described him as the "master of…bombastic kitsch."[70] In production style, he was almost the exact opposite of Bill Bottrell. Jackson, however, knew what he needed and what skills Foster brought to the table. For Jackson, the role of a producer wasn't to overtake the song; it was to help him achieve in very specific detail what he wanted. In the case of "Earth Song" he didn't need an overhaul, just small brush strokes.

Foster brought in talented orchestrator Bill Ross to

---

[68] David Foster recalls of his time working with Jackson: "He was always engaged and focused, and my biggest complaint is that he had a tendency to do dozens of takes of every song. I can't think past eight takes, so it made me crazy. I'm not one of those genius chess masters who are always thinking seventeen moves ahead, so I found that part of it more than a little frustrating." *Hitman: Forty Years Making Music, Topping Charts & Winning Grammys*, David Foster (with Pablo F. Fenjves) Pocket Books, 2008. Foster also worked with Jackson on "Childhood" and "Smile."

[69] Foster co-wrote the song "It's the Falling in Love" with Carole Bayer Sager.

[70] "Album Reviews: Kenny Loggins: *Vox Humana*." Don Shewey. *Rolling Stone*. June 6, 1985.

give the track a fuller, more powerful sound, most notably in the surging brass parts.[71] "The orchestra added so much drama," said assistant engineer, Rob Hoffman. "It made this beautiful song into an epic."[72]

Another important addition was Michael Thompson, a highly regarded session guitarist. Before Thompson, David Foster apparently offered the position to Eric Clapton, but either Clapton or Jackson (or both) passed on the idea. It is possible that Jackson remained concerned about Clapton's racist past.[73] Thompson, however (who had worked with David Foster and Quincy Jones), ended up being perfect for the job. His bluesy phrasings echo Jackson's pained singing

---

[71] Says assistant engineer Rob Hoffman: "I've worked with Bill Ross on my own productions specifically because of the incredible arrangement he did on that song."

[72] Author Interview with Rob Hoffman. June 2, 2011.

[73] While Clapton deeply admired and borrowed from black musicians, including Robert Johnson, Jimi Hendrix and Bob Marley, he also notoriously spoke of the importance of keeping Britain white. In a 1976 concert in Birmingham he said: "I used to be into dope, now I'm into racism. It's much heavier, man. Fucking wogs, man. Fucking Saudis taking over London. Bastard wogs. Britain is becoming overcrowded and Enoch will stop it and send them all back. The black wogs and coons and Arabs and fucking Jamaicans and fucking [indecipherable] don't belong here, we don't want them here. This is England. This is a white country. We don't want any black wogs and coons living here. We need to make clear to them they are not welcome. England is for white people, man. We are a white country." Clapton never apologized for these remarks.

beautifully.

A new mix of "Earth Song" was completed at the Hit Factory in 1994.[74] Most of Jackson's engineers assumed at that point that the track was finished. Although Jackson was pleased with many of the improvements, however, he still wasn't completely satisfied.

When recording moved back to Record One in Los Angeles in the spring of 1995, Jackson and his team focused in on the final details. Matt Forger estimated that around 40 multi-track tapes were used in total. "It crossed formats. It started on 24-track, switched to digital. The detail and work that went into it was staggering."[75]

Jackson turned to sonic magician, Bruce Swedien, to re-record parts of his lead vocal. To capture the immediacy and intensity Jackson wanted, Swedien recorded with a Neumann M-49 tube mike (instead of his usual SM7) and

---

[74] While still at the Hit Factory, Jackson wanted to re-record parts of his lead vocal on the track. The challenge, however, was matching his new vocals with the original ones. "We borrowed Bill [Bottrell's] U-47 mike and tried all of the Hit Factory's U-47's to see what matched, " recalls Rob Hoffman, "We eventually found one after a couple hours of listening." Later, they had to "fly in the EMT-250 reverb from the Hit Factory in New York, as it was used quite prominently in Bruce's original mix that he did in New York," recalls Rob Hoffman. "MJ wasn't satisfied with the Record One EMT's in this case. And he was right. We could all hear the difference." Author Interview with Rob Hoffman. May 24, 2011.
[75] Author Interview with Matt Forger. May 15, 2011.

had him get "as close as physically possible to the microphone, thereby eliminating almost all early reflections... I used no windscreen. I placed him as close as he could possibly get to this incredible old mike."[76] The results were subtle but palpable. "The real goal of music recording is to preserve the physical energy of the music and the musical statement itself," explains Swedien.[77]

Jackson saved the final ad libs for the last weekend of recording as he expected "to kill his voice" in the process. He told assistant engineers, Eddie Delena and Rob Hoffman, "I'm sorry, but I don't think any of us are going to sleep this weekend. There's a lot to get done, and we have to go to Bernie [Grundman for mastering] on Monday morning."[78]

Over the next few days, Jackson and a small crew of engineers ate, slept, and breathed the music. "He stayed at the studio the entire time," recalled Hoffman, "singing and mixing. I got to spend a couple quiet moments with him during that time. We talked about John Lennon one night as he was gearing up to sing the last vocal of the record—the huge ad libs at the end of 'Earth Song.' I told him the story of John singing 'Twist and Shout' while being sick, and though

---

[76] *In the Studio With Michael Jackson*. Bruce Swedien. Hal Leonard, 2009.
[77] *Ibid.*
[78] "Post here if you worked on Michael Jackson's *Dangerous* album." Rob Hoffman. Gearslutz Forum. June 27, 2009.

most people think he was screaming for effect, it was actually his voice giving out. He loved it, and then went in to sing his heart out."[79]

As was his custom, Jackson sang that night with all the lights out.[80] From the control room, Bruce Swedien and his crew of assistant engineers couldn't see anything. Yet what they heard roaring out of the darkness was astonishing: it was as if Jackson was channeling from the lungs of the earth—a pained, fierce, prophetic voice, giving utterance to the suffering of the world.

Those who witnessed it could feel the hair standing up on the back of their necks.[81]

---

[79] "Later that night," says Hoffman, "while mixing, everyone left the room so MJ could turn it up. This was a common occurrence during the mixes, and I was left in the room with ear plugs, and hands over my ears, in case he needed something. This particular night, all the lights were out and we noticed some blue flashes intermittently lighting up the room during playback. After a few moments we could see that one of the speakers (custom quad augspuergers) was shooting blue flames. MJ liked this and proceeded to push all the faders up."
"Post here if your worked on Michael Jackson's *Dangerous* album." Rob Hoffman. Gearslutz Forum. June 27, 2009.

[80] "He always insisted on the lights being out," says Bruce Swedien. "The human being is primarily a visual animal. Light is distracting. Michael hated lights when recording." Author Interview with Bruce Swedien. May 19, 2011.

[81] "I've recorded just about everyone in music," says legendary recording engineer Bruce Swedien, who has also worked with Duke Ellington, Paul McCartney, Mick Jagger, and Barbara Streisand, among others, "and Michael is number one."

A Musical Apocalypse

The final version of "Earth Song" was a six-and-a-half minute tour de force that presented the human condition (and the condition of all life) in dramatic panorama.[82]

In the beginning is sound: the pulsing rhythm of crickets and birdsong, the vibrant cacophony of night. It conjures a lush, natural setting—a tropical jungle or

---

[82] "It meant so much to Michael," says Matt Forger. "It all came together in an incredible way. Everything was realized as completely as possible." It was a testament not only to Jackson's abilities as a composer and singer, but as an assembler and director of an eclectic team of musicians, producers and engineers. "What Billy brought to it was amazing, what David brought to it was amazing, what Bruce brought to it was amazing," says Brad Buxer. "But it was Michael guiding the whole thing—his perfectionism, his chords and lyrics, his execution."

rainforest—brimming with life and music. "I believe in its primordial form all of creation is sound and that it's not just random sound, that it's music," Jackson once explained.[83]

A cascading harp opens the scene as the listener enters a sort of edenic paradise. The harp is inspired in part by composers like Debussy and Tchaikovsky (two of Jackson's favorites), both of whom made frequent use of the instrument to evoke dream-like worlds of wonder and enchantment. As a student of history and literature, Jackson was also no doubt well aware of the harp's rich symbolic import.[84] The opening represents the world at sunrise, the world in all its natural beauty, balance and diversity.

The ebullient mood evoked in these opening seconds, however, quickly transforms into something more ominous. A

---

[83] Robert E. Johnson. "Michael Jackson in Africa." *Ebony/Jet*. May 1992.

[84] In the Bible, the harp is often connected to David, King of Israel, composer of the Psalms, and probably the most renowned musician in the history of three major religions (Judaism, Christianity and Islam). In literature, the Aeolian harp—named after the ancient Greek god of the wind, Aeolus—symbolized the creative power of nature. When the wind blew, the music came. The Romantic poets frequently used the wind harp as a metaphor for the mysterious medium through which nature communed with the artist. The harp also represents spontaneity, wildness, and freedom. Its creative expression isn't calculated or premeditated. It isn't trying to be witty or ironic or important. It simply comes and is. Yet it also symbolizes transience. The music can leave as quickly and unexpectedly as it arrives.

deep, primal sound slowly encroaches "like an unfathered vapour that enwraps, at once, some lonely traveller."[85] Then comes the piano hook, the chords capturing a mixture of melancholy and longing.[86]

"What about sunrise, what about rain," Jackson sings, "What about all the things that you said we were to gain." His voice is world-weary, dejected as he assesses what's been lost in the name of "progress."

Sunrise and rain are symbols of natural renewal. In contrast, Jackson presents humanity's quest for short-sighted consumption, exploitation and "gain." In the opening lines, he is taking aim at the very foundations of modern society. "What have we done to the world?" he asks. "Look what we've done."

Beneath his vocal, a deep synth pad haunts like a shadow, its chords seemingly rising from the soil. His narration describes a world turned wasteland. "Did you ever stop to notice/ All the blood we shed before," Jackson sings, his voice quivering as it rises to falsetto, "Did you ever stop to notice/ This crying earth, these weeping shores."

With most singers such sentiments might come across

---

[85] William Wordsworth. *The Prelude, Book VI.* 1805.
[86] The tone here is akin to what Wordsworth once captured in "Tintern Abbey" as the "still, sad music of humanity." "Lines composed a few miles above Tintern Abbey on revisiting the banks of the Wye during a tour, 13 July 1798." 1798.

as cloying or melodramatic.[87] Yet Jackson had a unique capacity to inject words with weight—to make people feel them far beyond the way they look on a lyric sheet. As Marvin Gaye once put it: "Michael will never lose the quality that separates the merely sentimental from the truly heartfelt. It's rooted in the blues, and no matter what genre Michael is singing, that boy's got the blues."[88] In "Earth Song," Jackson is singing the blues on a cosmic scale.

With each verse, the music builds. The guitar reflects Jackson's anguished sentiments with soulful interjections. The majestic orchestration swells and subsides. The tambourine gives momentum to the chorus.

In the second verse, Jackson alludes to the peace that was "pledged" with "your only son" — seemingly turning his queries from humanity to God (or perhaps addressing the two as one). When will these promises of peace and redemption be fulfilled, he is asking. Later, he also references the prophet Abraham and the "promised land" that was covenanted to his descendants. These are Job-like remonstrations to deity. "I cry unto thee, and thou dost not hear me," Job lamented,

---

[87] Cover interpretations of the song tend to fall short not merely because of the difficulty of the vocal, but because of the depth and soul it requires.

[88] Michael Jackson: Commemorative Edition. *Rolling Stone.* July 2009.

Did not I weep for him that was in trouble?

Was not my soul grieved for the poor...

And now my soul is poured out upon me;

The days of affliction have taken hold upon me...

My harp also is turned to mourning,

And my organ into the voice of them that weep.[89]

Like an ancient poet-prophet, Jackson is "probing the limits of the Almighty," while posing profound questions on behalf of the wounded and abandoned.

At the heart of his lamentation is the age-old quandary of why the innocent must suffer ("Did you ever stop to notice/ All the children dead from war"). The tension of these unanswered entreaties builds through the verses before erupting into the pain-filled cries of the chorus.

Listen to the explosion of drums and earth-shaking bass after the second verse: this is the moment the song transforms from forlorn to righteous indignation. It is intended to rattle the foundations of power and stir the listener out of indifference. The second chorus takes on more force and momentum, gathering energy like a storm. The power is amplified by what sounds like the Heavenly host piercing the veil like sunrays through clouds.

Before the climax, however, comes one last moment

---

[89] The Holy Bible, King James Version. Job 30. New York: Oxford Edition: 1769.

of reflection. Jackson's voice is fragile and vulnerable again, no longer the howling representative of the voiceless. "Earth Song" is an excellent illustration of how versatile Jackson is vocally: it is a voice that "conjures the human in extremis"— extreme heights and depths, extreme vulnerability and power, despair and rage.[90] In the bridge alone, he moves from wonder-filled awe ("I used to dream/ I used to glance beyond the stars") to sudden panic and estrangement ("Now I don't know where we are") to utter despair and outrage ("although I know/ *we've drifted far!*"). This bridge represents a threshold moment, a liminal state between what was, or could be, and what is.[91]

Yet it is the epic climax that follows that pushes the song to new heights. The chorus cries unfold with greater and greater intensity. The air swirls with apocalyptic energy, "the tumult of mighty harmonies."[92] Jackson's voice is like Jeremiah ("the weeping prophet") in lamentation: "Are not all my words as fire...and a hammer that shatters rock?"[93] It is like Shelley's revolutionary call to the West Wind: "Drive my

---

[90] Music critic Mark Greif used this description for the voice of Radiohead's Thom Yorke. "Radiohead, or the Philosophy of Pop." n + 1. Issue 3. January 2006.

[91] As Jackson put it in "Wanna Be Startin' Somethin'": "You're stuck in the middle/ And the pain is thunder."

[92] "Ode to the West Wind." Percy B. Shelley.1820.

[93] The Holy Bible, King James Version. Jeremiah 23:29. New York: Oxford Edition: 1769.

dead thoughts over the universe,/ Like wither'd leaves, to quicken a new birth…scatter[ed] as from an unextinguish'd hearth/ Ashes and sparks…The trumpet of a prophecy!"[94]

His call and response with the Andraé Crouch Choir unleashes into the open air voices that have been smothered. With each plight Jackson brings to our attention, the choir reinforces with the recurring chant, *What about us!*

> What about yesterday? *(What about us!)*
> What about the seas? *(What about us!)*
> The heavens are falling down *(What about us!)*
> I can't even breathe *(What about us!)*

The "us" is the amplified voice of the "Other": all who have been silenced, marginalized, oppressed or disregarded. Jackson is witnessing with them and allowing them to witness for themselves. It is a massive civil rights demonstration set to music.

The power of the exchange between Jackson and the choir is simply astonishing. "What about the holy land?" he shouts, as the choir comes rushing behind like a torrent, (*"What about it!"*) "Torn apart by creed *(What about us!)*/ What about the common man? (*What about us!*)/ Can't we set him free (*What about us!*)/ What about children dying? (*What*

---

[94] "Ode to the West Wind." Percy B. Shelley.1820.

about us!)/ Can't you hear them cry? (*What about us!).*"

Then comes a slight deviation, as Jackson pleads: "*Where did we go wrong? Someone tell me why!*"

His voice conveys desperation and bewilderment. How did we get here? How can it be accepted? *Someone tell me why!*

Finally, as Jackson reaches the end of his litany— exhausted, but unrelenting—he shouts, "*Do we give a damn?*" before letting out wordless exclamations of anguish. Language simply can't do justice to the pain and suffering he is trying to express and bring to the world's attention. In the background, the chorus cries continue as Jackson soars over the top.

The term "apocalypse" is typically understood to mean the destruction that will take place in the "end of days." Yet in the original Greek it means a "lifting of the veil," a revelation or prophecy that helps humanity to see what is hiding in plain sight.

"Earth Song," according to this definition, is a musical apocalypse. It takes the listener from an imagined paradise of harmony and vitality to our present state of degradation and divisions. Its final question ("*Do we give a damn?*") is about apathy. Why do we passively accept the way things are? Why can't we see and stop the self-destruction? Why can't we imagine and work toward something better?

Rise From the Slumberous Mass

It is difficult to find parallels for "Earth Song" in popular music.[95] Bob Dylan's "A Hard Rain's a-Gonna Fall" offers a similarly prophetic, Biblically-rooted warning against self-destruction (including the threat of nuclear annihilation) that both speaks to its time and transcends it.[96]

Other "protest songs," of course, have included environmental themes: Marvin Gaye's "Mercy Mercy Me,"

---

[95] I asked Bill Bottrell if he could think of any musical precedents for "Earth Song." His response: "Thematically, perhaps 'What's Goin' On.' Musically, it's probably most comparable to 'Man in the Mirror.' But there is more rock in it. 'Man in the Mirror' was more R&B fused with gospel. Also, I think "Earth Song," because Michael wrote it, was in some ways more personal, more internalized. You can feel it in his delivery."

[96] Most critics, myself included, would agree that Dylan's song is lyrically superior. Jackson's, however, is a more original piece of music and a far more dynamic vocal performance.

Joni Mitchell's "Big Yellow Taxi" and Neil Young's "Natural Beauty" and "After the Goldrush," among others.[97] But these tracks were much more modest and conventional in presentation, fitting rather neatly in the genres of folk or soul.

In terms of cultural impact, one parallel for "Earth Song" is John Lennon's classic, "Imagine." Both songs became global anthems with instantly identifiable piano hooks and choruses. Both ask listeners to try to care for the world we have, rather than simply be placated by the thought of an afterlife. Yet where "Imagine" makes a subdued, elegant statement, "Earth Song" is epic, intense, and visceral. This, indeed, is one reason "Imagine" is more palatable to the average music listener. Its radical ideas can be softened by its ethereal sound. "Earth Song," in contrast, seeks to shatter indifference, as it demands accountability. Radio can't do it justice. It is a song that was created to blast out of speakers if it couldn't be seen live.

Stylistically, "Earth Song" combines elements of rock, opera, soul and gospel, but it is rooted in the sensibility of the blues. "He was the international emblem of the African American blues spiritual impulse that goes back through slavery," observes Dr. Cornel West. "Michael Jackson was part

---

[97] Interestingly, Jackson's longtime musical rival Prince recorded a song nearly a decade later with very similar themes entitled "Planet Earth" (2007). Like Jackson's track, it combines scriptural allusions with green politics to epic effect.

of that tremendous wave in the ocean of human expression."[98]

Indeed, the call and response form featured so prominently in "Earth Song" is a continuation of a long heritage in Black America that began with field hollers and spirituals.[99] "The core of gospel politics lies in the 'call and response' principle of African American culture," notes Craig Werner. "When the preacher or singer shapes a call, it is already a response to the shared suffering of the community. If the members of the congregation or audience recognize their own experiences in the call, they respond."[100]

In addition to giving voice to this "shared suffering," call and response has often been used as a form of resistance to oppression: by representing the voices of "the people" and their struggles, it allowed them to *perform* solidarity and gave them the strength to take action.[101] Nietzsche argued that it

---

[98] "Georgetown professor assesses Michael Jackson's cultural legacy." Cornel West. *The Tavis Smiley Show.* PBS. June 30, 2009.

[99] For context read W.E.B. Du Bois's chapter on the "sorrow songs" from *The Souls of Black Folk* (1900). Also, *Blues People* (1963) by Leroi Jones (Amiri Baraka).

[100] *A Change is Gonna Come: Music, Race and the Soul of America.* Craig Werner. University of Michigan Press, 2006.

[101] The communal dialogue in call and response is also a prominent feature in the choruses of Greek tragedies. In this context, it allows the community—and by extension the audience—to comment on the action of the "play" and thereby help construct its meaning. The chorus, in other words, invites the audience to participate in the unfolding drama.

was in the bosom of this Primal Unity that human beings found deliverance and redemption.[102] One's suffering could be transfused into communal, creative energy. Jackson uses call and response, then, both to demonstrate our dire predicament as well as to showcase how we might collectively harness suffering for productive ends.

While "Earth Song" is clearly inspired by the Bible, Jackson revises the Judeo-Christian notion that nature is fallen and must be tamed or dominated by men. He draws from nature-oriented Eastern religions, including Hinduism, Sufism, and Taoism as well as Paganism and the indigenous traditions of Africans and Native Americans to introduce a sensibility of cooperation and harmony, not hierarchy and domination. "The Earth we share is not just a rock tossed through space, but a living, nurturing being," he wrote. "She cares for us. She deserves our care in return."[103]

"Earth Song" is also grounded in a rich tradition of prophetic poetry: From William Blake ("O Earth O Earth

---

[102] See Nietzsche's *The Birth of Tragedy.*

[103] "This we know," wrote Chief Seattle in an eloquent 1852 letter to the United States Government. "The earth does not belong to man, man belongs to the earth. All things are connected like the blood that unites us all. Man did not weave the web of life, he is merely a strand in it. Whatever he does to the web, he does to himself." *The Power of Myth.* Joseph Campbell (With Bill Moyers). Anchor Books, 1991. p. 43.

return!...Rise from the slumberous mass")[104] to William Wordsworth ("I felt a sense of pain when I beheld/ The silent trees, and saw the intruding sky")[105]; From W.B. Yeats ("The blood-dimmed tide is loosed, and everywhere/ The ceremony of innocence is drowned")[106] to W.E.B. DuBois ("Still quivering at unrighted Wrong;/ His soul aflame, and on his lips/ A tale of prophecy and waiting Work.")[107]

In terms of dramatic form, "Earth Song" is perhaps best understood in the tradition of tragedies. Like Greek and Shakespearean tragedies, it dramatizes the human struggle against fate. Yet Jackson re-presents this struggle, not from the perspective of royalty or heroic figures, but from the planet itself—from life as a collective (highlighting the voices of the wounded, vulnerable and invisible).[108] In "Earth Song," then, Jackson isn't merely representing himself. He is acting as the medium for a modern tragedy: the struggle of earth and its inhabitants for survival against increasingly overwhelming odds.

---

[104] "Introduction." *Songs of Experience*. William Blake. 1794
[105] "Michael." William Wordsworth. 1798.
[106] "The Second Coming." W.B. Yeats. 1920.
[107] "The Passing of Douglass." W.E.B. DuBois. 1900.
[108] "In his heart, he carried other lifetimes," said Smokey Robinson, "It was more than having soul; it was soul that went deep into the soil of a whole people's history." Michael Jackson: Commemorative Edition. *Rolling Stone*. July 2009.

Over the Top

"Earth Song" was released as a single in November of 1995. Through much of the world, amazingly, it played on pop stations next to songs by the Spice Girls, Hootie and the Blowfish, and Take That. It reached #1 on the charts in fifteen countries. In the U.K., it became Jackson's biggest single ever, selling over a million copies. In Germany, similarly, it became Jackson's bestselling single, staying at #1 for five weeks and attaining platinum certification.

Strangely, however, it wasn't even released as a single in the United States. This absence is even more noteworthy considering Jackson's previous single, "You Are Not Alone," was a #1 hit in the U.S. Yet for unexplained reasons, it wasn't offered to radio or record stores in America. Producer Bill Bottrell feels the decision wasn't by accident. "[The song] was anti-corporate, anti-nature-raping," he says. "So it was prone to censorship."[109] Even if it wasn't officially blocked, the fact that it wasn't seen as viable for U.S. listeners is telling.

Meanwhile, the response from critics was mostly dismissive. Reviews described it as "over the top," "bathetic," "cloying" and "sentimental." *Rolling Stone* wrote it off as a "showpiece...something with which to knock 'em dead in Monte Carlo."[110] Others scoffed about its concern for trees and whales and elephants.

Such assessments were indicative of the critical and cultural sensibilities of the time. Rock critics despised few things more in the 1990s than "sincerity." An earnest, socially conscious effort simply didn't have a chance in a decade dominated by cynicism, apathy, and irony. The days of social projects like USA for Africa, Live Aid and rainforest preservation were not only over, but remembered scornfully as celebrity vanity vehicles. A 1998 Stanford University study showed that malaise and cynicism was on the rise for all age groups.[111] It no longer seemed plausible from this sensibility

---

[109] Author Interview with Bill Bottrell. May 14, 2011.

[110] "Michael Jackson's *HIStory*." James Hunter. *Rolling Stone*. August 1995.

[111] "Generation X not so special: Malaise, Cynicism on the Rise." News Release. August 1998.

that art (especially popular music) could speak to big problems.[112]

By the end of the Reagan/Bush/Thatcher era Generation X had had enough. It had a hard time believing in anything. Its angst was near-ubiquitous (thus, the appeal of grunge and gangsta rap). Yet Gen-X's disillusionment also prevented it from exploring many of the roots of this angst— or from looking beyond the narrow borders of its immediate existence. The music, in many cases, simply glorified, perpetuated and sold packaged rebellion and nihilism. Not until the late 1990s and early 2000s did environmental issues (and other causes related to globalization, social injustice and non-violence) begin to receive major attention again from young people.

The earnestness and ambition of "Earth Song" in addressing such problems, then, was in many ways anachronistic. The general public, particularly in a privileged country like the U.S., in the midst of an economic boom, preferred staring at its own reflection to looking outward.

The disdain for "Earth Song" also spoke to the

---

[112] When Jackson started work on "Earth Song" in the late 1980s the zeitgeist was very different. Wrote Stephen Holden in 1987 for the *New York Times*: "Ever since "We Are the World," the all-star U.S.A. for Africa charity single and album two and a half years ago that launched a rash of charitable pop causes, there has been a movement within pop's higher artistic echelons to make music that addresses humane concerns." That movement continued for another few years before fading in the early 1990s.

general herd mentality in music journalism.[113] In this case, the knee-jerk consensus was that the song's theme, size and scope automatically equated to "pompous" and "bombastic." Few critics were able to actually consider the song on its own terms. No one, after all, would expect Queen to sound like Bob Dylan. "Earth Song" was big and dramatic because it was intended to be big and dramatic.

Yet it was clear that the biggest problem for critics was Michael Jackson himself. Since the mid-1980s, the media had developed a simple, but profitable portrait of Jackson that could be cut and pasted into each new story: He was a naïve, strange, out-of-touch megalomaniac. Reviews of his music are almost universally interpreted through this lens beginning in the late 1980s, regardless of the merits of the song or album. Jackson, they often argued, should stick to the blissful "dance music" of *Off the Wall* and *Thriller*, rather than some of the "angry," "defiant," "political" material that followed. Critics always preferred to view Jackson as an entertainer rather than an artist (a stereotype with a long racial history of which Jackson was well aware). As his music became more experimental and challenging, journalists tried in vain to put

---

[113] As Anthony DeCurtis observes: "Much rock writing is snotty, adolescent, and dismissive...Rock critics have routinely aspired to supplanting their subjects, and they've succeeded at least in their own work and their own minds, if nowhere else." Anthony DeCurtis. Foreword. *Reading Rock and Roll*, Ed. Kevin H. Dettmar. Columbia University Press, 1999.

him "back in his place." They didn't want to hear songs about racism, media distortion, war and the environment, they said. They wanted a "return to basics."[114]

---

[114] In 2003, Björk did an *In Camera* interview at showstudio. One of the questions came from none other than Michael Jackson. Their brief exchange not only reveals a deep respect for each other's artistry and the inspiration both drew from nature, but some astute observations on Jackson's fraught relationship with American critics and journalists.

MICHAEL JACKSON: I have always loved and admired your creativity. Nature's struggle to survive alongside mankind has been an inspiration for me: given the natural beauty of your Icelandic homeland, how does nature inspire your work?

BYöRK: I hope this doesn't sound too naff, but being alone in nature, especially after walking for hours, just puts you in your place and you realize how small you are and how plenty of everything is all around you. Then you just let go and surrender, become part of it. I'm so chuffed you asked me a question! I have to say you're the best, keep fighting and it angers me how cruel everybody is to you. It's like in the US right now it's illegal to be an eccentric. Maybe people would have been more understanding if you were a contemporary of Ludwig II of Bavaria, who commissioned Wagner and lived with the swans. I listen to "Butterflies" off your last album all the time. You are a true artist! Thanks for fighting and believing in magic even though the rest of the world have forgotten about it."

The Body as Canvas

Jackson's performances of "Earth Song" were likewise the subject of considerable controversy and scorn. Many critics interpreted them as the perfect illustration of Jackson's messiah complex. Others were bothered by the visceral effect the performances had on crowds (audience members are often shown in concerts reaching out for Jackson and sobbing).

In the brief four years the song was performed (1995-1999), it served as the dramatic climax to Jackson's shows.[115] They were remarkable spectacles. Regardless of one's estimation of the song, watching him sing, stomp, howl, dangle precariously over the crowd, and pour out his soul on

---

[115] Jackson also rehearsed the song in preparation for his *This Is It* concert series at the O2 Arena in London. However, he never had the opportunity to perform it to a live audience again after 1999.

stage, at least made it clear why he was one of the most powerful artists of the modern era.[116] It was a potent blend of entertainment and art, prophecy and activism, music and visuals, carried out in a way that had never been done before.

The richness of these performances is only beginning to be properly contextualized and understood. "Jackson," writes acclaimed visual artist Constance Pierce,

> is often dramatically illuminated, while engulfed in a Baroque convolution of drapery, and raised high against the night sky on a 'cherry-picker' apparatus. Hovering above his massive audience, the illuminated drapery of his silken cape unfurling, Jackson's mesmerizing presence gathers thousands below him into a participatory aesthetic, a 'performance art' ritual...Candles are lit and a torrent of arms lifts in unison. The gesture of passion embodied in Jackson's performance of 'Earth Song,' both iconic and

---

[116] In a performance at Olympic Stadium in Seoul, Korea on October 13, 1996, a young male Korean fan somehow managed to elude security and climb up onto the cherry picker as it hovered high over the audience during the climax of "Earth Song." Jackson seemed shocked at first, but alertly grabbed hold of the fan to prevent him from falling. For the remainder of the song, Jackson clutches the fan tightly as he continues singing. When the cherry picker came back down to the stage, the fan was torn away by several security guards. The performance can be seen on YouTube.

transcendent, burns itself into the collective consciousness of the 20th century.[117]

This evocative description of the iconic, ritualistic, participatory nature of Jackson's performances gives a sense of what made them so transcendent and unifying for audiences.

Yet for all the pageantry and theatricality, it was the song itself and Jackson's ability to inject it with soul and passion that gave his performances such force. In perhaps his most stripped down rendition of the song at a one-off concert in Brunei in July of 1996, glistening with sweat at the conclusion of a three-hour show, Jackson delivers an impromptu coda (*"Tell me what about it!"*) that ranks among his finest moments on stage. There are no props, no pyrotechnics—just him, the mic, and the music.

The "messianic" charge gained more currency, however, after a performance at the 1996 BRIT Awards. In the middle of Jackson's biblically-inflected presentation, Pulp singer Jarvis Cocker stormed the stage and pulled his pants down to protest what he perceived as Jackson's "offensive" Christ-like imitation. Cocker was subsequently arrested and questioned by police about potentially injuring several child

---

[117] "Lacrymae Rerum: Reflections of a Visual Artist Informed and Inspired By Gestures of Transcendence in the Passionate Art of Michael Joseph Jackson." *Passions of the Skies in Fine Arts Expression.* International Society of Phenomenology. Fine Arts and Aesthetics 16th Annual Conference. Harvard University. May 18, 2011.

performers caught up in the incident. He was eventually
released without charge. [118]

Jackson did indeed seem to be playing a messiah
figure in the performance. What is strange is that so many
people, including Jarvis Cocker, interpreted the performance
so literally. Cocker was celebrated by hipster journalists and
some fellow alternative musicians (including Oasis) for his
"brave" act (*Melody Maker* went so far as to say he should be
"knighted"). Yet in retrospect it is Cocker's sanctimonious
defense of Jesus that seems silly and egotistical. Jackson was
using messianic gestures and symbols not because he literally
thought he was the messiah, but because of what tapping into
that archetype could express and communicate artistically. As
a dancer and performance artist, his body acted as his canvas.
"Embodying" the song meant becoming whatever the music
and lyrics dictated to him. With this particular show, it was

---

[118] In a statement, Cocker said that his "actions were a form of
protest at the way Michael Jackson sees himself as some Christ-like
figure with the power of healing." Jackson released his own
statement through Epic Records, which read: "Michael Jackson
respects Pulp as artists but is totally shocked by their behavior and
utterly fails to understand their complete lack of respect for fellow
artists and performers. His main concern is for the people that
worked for him and the fact that children should be attacked. He
feels sickened, saddened, shocked, upset, cheated, angry but is
immensely proud that the cast remained professional and the show
went on despite the disgusting and cowardly behavior of the two
characters that tried to disrupt it."

the best way he felt he could convey the song's agony, suffering and redemption.[119]

---

[119] "When Jackson embodies a particular archetypal stance," notes Constance Pierce, "his physical body transfigures into a kind of symbolic, elegant calligraphy wherein the Divine may channel gestures of explosive emotion or intimate compassion. The artist becomes shamanic, taking on our massive cumulative 'shadow' and sweeping it whole into the light. "Lacrymae Rerum: Reflections of a Visual Artist Informed and Inspired By Gestures of Transcendence in the Passionate Art of Michael Joseph Jackson." *Passions of the Skies in Fine Arts Expression*. International Society of Phenomenology. Fine Arts and Aesthetics 16th Annual Conference. Harvard University. May 18, 2011.

Crying in the Wilderness

Criticisms of Jackson's short film for "Earth Song," directed by talented fine art photographer, Nick Brandt, followed similar lines of reasoning as criticisms directed at his performances.[120] Jackson, they said, was pretending he had the power to magically solve all the world's problems. Did he

---

[120] Jackson first reached out to Indian director, Tarsem Singh, best known at the time for his music videos for R.E.M. ("Losing My Religion") and Deep Forest ("Sweet Lullaby"). Jackson was enamored by the latter video, which featured a young girl riding a tricycle among various cultures around the globe. The video was nominated for several awards. According to Singh, Jackson's people contacted him about directing a video for "Earth Song," but he responded that he wasn't interested. Eventually he ended up listening to the song and to his surprise, he loved it. The collaboration reportedly fell through, however, after Singh refused to film Jackson's face in the video. Singh's loss ended up being Nick Brandt's gain. *I Want My MTV: The Uncensored Story About the Music Video Revolution.* Craig Marks and Rob Tannenbaum. Dutton, 2011.

really believe healing the planet was that simple?

This reading, however, again fails to move beyond the most reactionary literalism. In "Earth Song" Jackson is actually deconstructing Western mythology about progress and "civilization." The short film was shot in four different locations around the world: the Amazon rainforest, a field in Tanzania, a war zone in Croatia, and a burnt-down forest in New York.[121] In the video he is depicted in a similar position as everyone else, surrounded by the repercussions of human greed and violence. The earth has become a wasteland.

"His grimaces are stark affectations of remorse, fear, anger and determination," notes film critic Armond White. "He's doing something almost miraculous—dramatizing hubris for the purpose of enlightening and improving life for others…His stance, holding on to tree limbs while buffeted by the winds of fate, is not sacrificial, it's not a crucifixion—it's a *positioning*. Michael is staking his beliefs in where and how we live."[122] White's analysis is astute. Jackson's positioning in the short film is about identification.

---

[121] Some of the imagery in Jackson's short film and performances bears resemblance to a Soviet propaganda film entitled "Ava Maria" (Ivan Ivanov-Vano, 1971) which protests U.S. imperialism in relation to the Vietnam War. It is unknown whether Jackson was familiar with this film and used it as inspiration for the visual presentation of "Earth Song."

[122] *Keep Moving: The Michael Jackson Chronicles*. Resistance Works. 76-79.

After showing images of deforestation, pollution, death, and cruelty, Jackson (along with small groups of people from other parts of the world) drops to his knees, digging his fists into the soil in desperate supplication. It is this symbolic gesture that begins an imagined reversal. Only by caring about the Earth's (and the Other's) pain, by understanding how we are connected, and by our collective will for change, can we hope to heal the world.[123]

The film, then, is about contrasts: the world as it is and the world as it could be. While Jackson is at the center of the film, he is not portrayed as a "messiah," but rather as "the voice of one crying in the wilderness."

---

[123] "The most interesting time for me [working on *Earth Song*]," recalls director Nick Brandt, "was when I had a bunch of very cynical jaded New Yorkers for crew, for the part of the shoot that he was in. And they were just, 'Oh yeah, Michael Jackson, da-da-da-da-da…' But then when he started singing at the end of that song, and he's just screaming out the vocals… you could just see, you just look around and everybody had stopped in their tracks and was watching him, riveted. And he'd only give me one take from each angle because he was blasted by these wind machines and stuff was flying in his eyes. I mean, it's really hard, I mean firing dust and leaves and all manner of stuff into his face. And everybody was just electrified. He completely turned everybody around."

Legacy

Nearly eighteen years since it was first released, "Earth Song" remains overlooked by most critics.[124] While the great social protests of Bob Dylan, John Lennon and Marvin Gaye are rightfully recognized among *Rolling Stone's* Top 5 songs of all time, Michael Jackson's "Earth Song" doesn't even

---

[124] Since Jackson's death in 2009 it *has* received some attention from academics, including essays by Willa Stillwater, Constance Pierce, and Gerd Buschmann. Such in-depth analyses from a variety of academic fields will allow "Earth Song" to be contextualized and interpreted in ways critics failed to do upon its release. (Gerd Buschmann's essay was published in German. "Der Sturm Gottes zur Neuschöpfung: Biblische Symboldidaktik in Michael Jacksons Mega-Video-Hit Earth Song. Katechetische Blätter. Vol. 121, no. 3, pp.187-196. 1996.)

crack the Top 500. Indeed, the song is rarely even acknowledged among *Jackson's* best songs.

Still, in spite of the critical neglect, "Earth Song" has gained admirers over the years for its prescience and power. "I'm still very proud of it," reflects producer Bill Bottrell. "There is nothing else like it in terms of size and structure...It has the broadest scope, the most unusual blend of elements...It expresses such deeply felt, powerful emotions." Film critic Armond White praises the *Earth Song* video as being among "the most magnificent combinations of music and imagery in the centenary of motion pictures."[125]

Following Jackson's death in 2009, a resurgence of interest in the artist led many back to this unusual anthem and its haunting cry on behalf of the planet. It suddenly dawned on some people that long before terms like climate change, carbon emissions and "going green" became part of mainstream discourse, Michael Jackson was sounding the alarm, not only for the environment, but numerous other pressing social and political issues. In the 1990s, he was arguably the most influential global spokesperson for environmentalism.

In recent years, "Earth Song" has been performed on popular shows like *American Idol*, *The X Factor*, and the Grammy Awards, among others. It has also been performed

---

[125] *Keep Moving: The Michael Jackson Chronicles*. Resistance Works. 76-79.

by symphonies around the world, from London to Japan. Globally, it continues to be one of his most beloved works.

Yet beyond its artistic merit, perhaps its most substantial legacy is in the ways it has raised awareness and prompted individual and social change. As Jackson himself said in 2009, he wanted the song to "open up people's consciousness."[126] He didn't want his audiences to simply feel bad; he wanted them to act. And that is precisely what many have done.

Numerous educators now use "Earth Song" in classes to bring awareness to environmental, human and animal rights issues. Green bloggers and organizers use it to draw interest to environmental activities and causes, particularly among young people. In 2010, a panel at the Schomburg Center for Research in Black Culture was dedicated to Jackson's song and its value and resonance to people of color.[127] Jackson's global fan base, meanwhile, is pushing to make "Earth Song" the official anthem of Earth Day.

"Earth Song" has also inspired activism. "After seeing the 'Earth Song' segment of *This Is It*," says Trisha Franklin,

---

[126] Michael Jackson's *This Is It*. DVD. Sony Pictures, 2010.

[127] "Black Ain't Green: Honoring Michael's Environmental Consciousness and Philanthropic Endeavors." Schomburg Center for Research in Black Culture.
http://www.nypl.org/audiovideo/black-ain%E2%80%99t-green-honoring-michael%E2%80%99s-environmental-consciousness-and-philanthropic-endeav. June 5, 2010.

"I felt absolutely compelled to do something to help, as Michael asked. So I started a project to plant trees all over the world in Michael's name. 'A Million Trees For Michael' now has over 13,000 fans on Facebook and we get thousands of hits a month on our website. We have planted over 20,000 trees in the world and are hoping to plant thousands more."[128]

"Earth Song's" call-to-arms continues to inspire new generations. After seeing the *Earth Song* music video, one sensitive ten-year-old named Draven was so profoundly moved he pledged to tell everyone he knew about its message. He hadn't known about most of the issues the video portrayed and told his grandmother it "made him realize how important it is to take care of the earth."[129]

---

[128] Author Interview with Trisha Franklin. June 1, 2011.

[129] Author Interview with Mary House. June 4, 2011. The parents of a three-year-old girl tell a similar story. One day they stumbled upon Jackson's video on YouTube. "[Our daughter] was profoundly moved," writes her mother, Danika Carter. "The first time I saw the video myself I was concerned that [my husband] was showing this to our then [three-year-old]…I was concerned that she was too young to see it, to understand its message and to see the pain and sadness. But I was wrong. This was the day my [daughter] became an environmentalist. She was so moved by the video that she kept asking me why the people were so sad, and why people hurt the animals and the earth. It was a wonderful opportunity to talk to her about how the decisions we make affect the environment, animals, and our community." "Teaching Children To Honor the Earth." http://www.drgreene.com/perspectives/2011/03/16/teaching-children-honor-earth. March 16, 2011.

Such stories may seem insignificant given the scope and complexity of the problems confronting the world. But they are seeds. They represent resistance to a trajectory that Jackson recognized as not only unjust and unwise but unsustainable.

An Adventure of Humanity

Michael Jackson performed "Earth Song" to a live audience for the final time on June 27, 1999 in Munich, Germany.

The show was the second of two Jackson-organized benefit concerts (the first took place in Seoul, Korea) entitled "Michael Jackson & Friends – An Adventure of Humanity." All the proceeds—an estimated $3.3 million dollars—were donated to the Nelson Mandela Children's Fund, the Red Cross, UNESCO, and Kosovo refugees.

The day of the concert in Munich was scorching hot. Fans were given water to prevent dehydration.[130] In the early

---

[130] Michael Jackson Fan Club. News Archives. June 1999.

afternoon, the show got underway with performances by Luther Vandross, Ringo Starr, and Andrea Bocceli, among others.

As the sun faded and the air cooled, however, the anticipation began to build for Michael Jackson. Munich Olympic Stadium was now packed to the brim, a sea of humanity converged from all corners of the world.

Jackson hit the stage shortly after 11:00pm. As he stood motionless, *David*-like, amidst smoke and a flood of light, the excitement of the crowd was palpable. This was the moment they had been waiting for. Jackson proceeded into a high-octane lineup of songs, including a smooth, deftly choreographed medley of "Dangerous" and "Smooth Criminal."

After finishing the set, Jackson ran back stage for a costume change and Gatorade while the elaborate backdrop was being built for his final number: "Earth Song."

During the break, Beethoven's "Ode to Joy" blared triumphantly through the warm summer air as lights surged through the crowd. Then, on the Jumbotron, a spinning globe appeared. The ecstatic mood suddenly turned contemplative as the moody, cosmic opening to "Earth Song" emanated through the stadium, followed by the mournful piano chords.

Jackson walks back onto the stage to the distant screams of fans, but mentally, one can tell, he is now inside his song.

He is dressed in black pants and a tattered black and

red overshirt. His face is pale. He looks fragile and somber. "*What about sunrise…*" The unmistakable tenor sends a frisson through the crowd.

His gestures are expressive, dramatic, intended to communicate to the furthest audience member. On the screen, scenes of destruction are projected while Jackson stalks the stage restlessly.

As the song progresses, the tension gradually builds. Jackson's body crouches, pulses, and sways. He is channeling the painful emotions of the song. The chorus swells and releases like surging waves.

While Jackson sings, a huge steel bridge is erected on stage in three connecting parts. It was an addition to the number that had only been done once before, just a few days earlier in Seoul. The concept was intended as a sort of "Bridge of No Return": refugees are seen crossing over to what they can only hope will be safety and freedom. After they pass, Jackson runs up the bridge himself. Pyrotechnics explode on both sides, simulating the attack of jets dropping bombs from overhead. Guitarist, Slash, meanwhile, plays a tempestuous guitar solo below, heightening the sense of chaos.

Engulfed in a cloud of smoke, Jackson stomps and shouts, "*Someone tell me why!*"

Then the unexpected happens. After a series of explosions, the middle part of the bridge Jackson is standing on suddenly dislodges, rises, and then drops nearly sixty feet.

"From my angle, I couldn't see what happened, so I

kept playing," recalls music director, Brad Buxer. "I could sense something was kind of strange, but I still heard Michael singing. When the smoke cleared, I saw the bridge had collapsed."[131]

Jackson's makeup artist, Karen Faye, said her "heart stopped beating" when she realized what happened. "Unlike rehearsals, and the last show [in Korea], [the bridge] didn't pause at its pinnacle," she remembers. "Instead it came careening down, gaining speed, with Michael tightly grasping the railings—still singing. I started screaming, but I could not even hear my own voice over the pyro, music, and the audience...From our vantage point we had lost sight of Michael...I could not imagine how [he] could have survived such a fall."[132]

The bridge landed with a thud in the orchestra pit in front of the stage.[133] Amazingly, while Jackson was shaken by

---

[131] Author Interview with Brad Buxer. June 12, 2011. Buxer adds: "It's incredible what Michael did that night. Any lesser performer would have stopped. He was pretty shaken, but he refused to cut the performance short."

[132] "What More Can I Give." Karen Faye. *Karen Faye – A Life Intersected.* July 27, 2010. Jackson, it should be noted, was lip synching to a backing track for this particular performance. Still, the fact that he survived the fall and continued performing is quite remarkable.

[133] According to Brad Buxer, the fall might have been much worse if not for an alert tech who helped slow the velocity of the falling bridge by getting some resistance on the cables.

the fall, he continued performing. The crowd in the front was stunned, but most of the audience simply assumed it was part of the show. Techs quickly jumped down to check on Jackson, but before they reached him, he was crawling back up onto the stage.

"I saw one arm reach for the floor of the stage," recalls Karen Faye, "then a long lean leg, another arm, another leg...He was up, center stage, finishing the end of 'Earth Song'! My mouth dropped open in relieved amazement."[134]

Concert organizer Briton Rikki Patrick, later tried to offer an explanation for what happened. "We think a cable must have snapped or something. It was really frightening. People in the audience were screaming and crying. Security men were running everywhere. It must have been terrifying for Michael. But he managed to scramble back on stage. He staggered off to one side where I was standing and collapsed on to a chair. I could see he was in a lot of pain and bleeding at the back of his head."[135]

After the show, Jackson was rushed to Rechts Der Isar Hospital in Munich. He sustained a serious injury to his back and bruises. Yet before being whisked to the hospital, he insisted on not only finishing "Earth Song," but also the

[134] "What More Can I Give." Karen Faye. *Karen Faye – A Life Intersected*. July 27, 2010.
[135] "Star Goes Down in a Blaze of Fire as Prop Collapses." *Daily Record*. June 29, 1999.

encore, "You Are Not Alone." The only thing he heard in his head, he later said, was his father's voice saying, "Michael, don't disappoint the audience!"[136]

After climbing back onto the stage from the dismantled bridge, surrounded by clouds of smoke, Jackson lets out his final exclamations. *Whoooo! Whoooo! Whoooo!*

Finally, with a single spotlight shining down, he stretches out his arms and looks out at the audience, drenched in sweat and depleted.

---

[136] "What More Can I Give." Karen Faye. *Karen Faye – A Life Intersected*. July 27, 2010.

Performance Art

This might have been the end. Yet during the second leg of the *HIStory Tour* Jackson added a denouement. Just as the dust settles, a tank comes rumbling out onto the stage.

In the background, militant drums play over portentous strings. The tank is rolling toward the audience, but before it reaches them, Jackson jumps out in front, modeling the iconic imagery of Tiananmen Square. He is *performing* civil resistance—literally placing himself and his art against an imposing symbol of power and destruction. It beautifully emblemizes the meaning and purpose of "Earth Song."

A soldier then arises from the machine and points a

gun at the refugees and Jackson. The audience gasps. He points it directly at Jackson's head as Jackson stares calmly back at him. The soldier has been trained to kill, but now, at the decisive moment he hesitates.

Unsettled, he nonetheless stands his ground, still aiming his gun at his unknown enemy. Then, from the side of the stage, a refugee child emerges. In tattered clothes, he walks toward the soldier carrying a flower. It is a symbol of life in all of its fragility, beauty and transience.

The soldier begins to come to his senses. He puts down his gun and takes off his helmet and goggles. As he looks into the boy's eyes, he drops to his knees and weeps.

The soldier and boy embrace, as do Jackson and the soldier. It is a scene of redemption and healing. In the background, sublime piano flourishes cascade like sheets of summer rain. The world may be filled with untold suffering and horror, yet here, Jackson demonstrates, is proof that there are still pockets of love, beauty, and music.

Flanked by the soldier, the child, and a group of refugees, he turns to his audience one final time, stretches out his arms, and tilts his head toward the sky.

Epilogue

Michael Jackson expected "Earth Song" to be the most important piece of his *This Is It* concert series in London. He created an entirely updated concept for the number, including an introductory 3D film.[137] While he never saw it realized, his children introduced a tribute rendition at the 2010 Grammy Awards.[138] "Through all his songs, his

---

[137] The 3D short featured a young girl (played by Jasmine Alveran) who falls asleep in a forest, only to wake up to a burned down wasteland. 3D glasses were made available do the audience and to viewers at home via retailer Target.

[138] This tribute was introduced by "We Are the World" co-writer Lionel Richie and sung by Smokey Robinson, Usher, Jennifer Hudson, Carrie Underwood and Celine Dion. After the performance, Jackson's three children accepted a "Lifetime Achievement Award" on behalf of their father. Said Grammy producer Ken Ehrlich of the choice to use "Earth Song" of all the hits in his catalog to pay tribute to Jackson: "This felt to us like it was really a way of representing him. It's like a tip of the hat. This song was so important to him." "Michael Was Complex: Ken Ehrlich Discusses the Grammys' 3-D Tribute to Jackson." Todd Martens. *Pop & Hiss* Music Blog. *The Los Angeles Times*. January 20, 2010.

message was simple: Love," said Jackson's oldest son, Prince. "Our father was always concerned about the planet and humanity ... We will continue to spread his message and help the world."[139]

"Earth Song" was the last song Jackson rehearsed before he died.

---

[139] "Michael Jackson 'Earth Song' Tribute Focuses on His Love of the Planet." Shaheem Reid. MTV.com.
http://www.mtv.com/news/articles/1630895/michael-jackson-grammy-tribute-focuses-on-his-love-planet.jhtml. January 31, 2010.

Earth Song Facts

RECORDED: 1989-1990, 1995 (Westlake Studio and
Record One – Los Angeles); 1994-1995 (The Hit Factory –
New York City)

CONTRIBUTORS: Written and Composed by Michael
Jackson; Produced by Michael Jackson, Bill Bottrell, and
David Foster; Lead Vocal by Michael Jackson; Choir: Andrae
Crouch Singers Choir; Bass: Guy Pratt; Guitar: Michael
Thompson; Piano: Bill Bottrell and David Paich;
Tambourine: Bill Bottrell; Orchestration: Jorge del Barrio and
Bill Ross; Synth Programming: Steve Porcaro and David
Paich; Engineering: Bill Bottrell and Bruce Swedien; Assistant
Engineers: Rob Hoffman and Eddie Delena; Mixing: Bernie
Grundman

RELEASED: November 27, 1995

CHART PERFORMANCE: Australian Singles Chart (#15); Austrian Singles Chart (#2); Belgian Singles Chart (#1); Dutch Singles Chart (#1); Eurochart Hot 100 Singles (#4); Finnish Singles Chart (#1); French Singles Chart (#2); German Singles Chart (#1); Italian Singles Chart (#6); New Zealand Singles Chart (#4); Norwegian Singles Chart (#4); Spanish Singles Chart (#1); Swedish Singles Chart (#4); Swiss Singles Chart (#1); UK Singles Chart (#1)

RECORDS/ACHIEVEMENTS: Six weeks at #1 in the U.K. Five weeks at #1 in Germany. Certified platinum in the U.K. and Germany. In both countries it is Jackson's most successful single. Reached #1 on the Eurochart Hot 100 singles in 2009, nearly fifteen years after it was first released. Received a Genesis Award for animal sensitivity in 1995. Music video nominated for a Grammy Award (Best Music Video, Short Form) in 1997.

NOTABLE PERFORMANCES: Wetten Dass..? (November 4, 1995); Brit Awards (February 19, 1996); World Music Awards (May 8, 1996); Royal Brunei Concert (July 16, 1996); Seoul, South Korea Concert – Fan on the Cherry Picker (October 13, 1996); Munich, Germany Concert – Bridge Collapse (June 27, 1999)

SHORT FILM: Directed by Nick Brandt; Filmed at the Amazon Rainforest, Carlovac, Croatia, Tanzania, and Warwick, New York.

NOTABLE COVERS: London Symphony Orchestra; Mandolin Orchestra; Ne-Yo and Charice; Haley Reinhart; Melanie Amaro

ESTIMATED COPIES SOLD: 7 million

Earth Song Timeline

June 1988: Michael Jackson conceives of "Earth Song" in his hotel room in Vienna, Austria.

July 1989: Michael Jackson begins working on "Earth Song" at Westlake Recording Studio D with producer Bill Bottrell.

October 1991: Michael Jackson decides to pass up "Earth Song" for the final lineup of *Dangerous*, feeling it is not quite "ready."

January 1994: Michael officially begins work on the *HIStory* album, pulling Bottrell's stem tape out of the vault.

March 1995: Michael Jackson finishes the final ad libs for "Earth Song" and "locks it in cement."

November 1995: "Earth Song" is released worldwide as the third single from *HIStory*. By the end of the year it has reached #1 in over fifteen countries, but nonetheless goes unreleased in the United States.

November 1995: Two days after the single is released, Michael Jackson performs "Earth Song" for the first time on the popular German TV Show "Wetten, dass..?"

December 1995: "Earth Song" stays at the top of the charts in Great Britain for six weeks, holding off the Beatles' first single in twenty-five years ("Free As a Bird"). "Earth Song" becomes his bestselling single in the U.K., selling an estimated 1.2 million copies.

February 1996: Michael Jackson performs "Earth Song" at the Brit Awards in London. The performance is marred by controversy when Pulp singer Jarvis Cocker storms the stage to protest Jackson's messianic symbolism.

June 1999: Eleven years after it was conceived, Michael Jackson performs "Earth Song" to a live audience for the final time in Munich, Germany. The performance is remembered for the bridge collapse that resulted in Jackson being rushed to the hospital.

June 2009: "Earth Song" is the final song Jackson rehearses at the Staples Center in Los Angeles, California. He is declared dead the next day, June 25, 2009.

June 2011: The first edition of *Earth Song: Inside Michael Jackson's Magnum Opus* is published.

Acknowledgments

I want to express my profound appreciation to Bill Bottrell, Michael Jackson's trusted friend, producer, and primary collaborator on "Earth Song." Your work with Michael will live as long as people listen to music. Thank you for the great conversations and fascinating stories about how this song came into being. I also want to thank Matt Forger, Bruce Swedien, Brad Buxer, Jorge del Barrio, Rob Hoffman, and Karen Faye for your time, memories and insights. This book wouldn't have been possible without each of you.

I express my sincere gratitude to Constance Pierce for your inspiration, wisdom and encouragement. Thank you to Armond White for speaking truth to power when few others had the courage. Thank you to Anna Dorfman for your generosity, artistic eye and a beautiful cover design. Thank you to Seven Bowie for your outstanding research and archives. And thank you to the Michael Jackson Estate for your kind support and assistance.

I also want to offer my heartfelt thanks to the MJJ Justice Project team, the Michael Jackson Fan Club, the Michael Jackson Tribute Portrait, the Michael Joseph Jackson Community, Fans United for MJ, Pay Michael Forward, Positively Michael, and Dancing With the Elephant for your support of my work. A special thanks also to Spike Lee, Dr. Mark Anthony Neal, Dr. Michael Eric Dyson, Deborah Ffrench, Dr. Willa Stillwater, Dr. Nina Fonoroff, Joie Collins, David Edwards, Chris Merante, Vera Matz, Reverend Catherine Gross, Lauren Trainor, Tricia Franklin, Mary House and Draven, for your valuable perspectives and contributions to Jackson's legacy. And finally, thank you to my family for your unfailing love and belief in me.

A Chat With Joe Vogel About Earth Song

From *Dancing With the Elephant: Conversations About Michael Jackson, His Art and Social Change.* Dr. Willa Stillwater and Joie Collins. 29 September 2011.

Joie: Willa and I are very happy to be joined by Joe Vogel this week. As you all know, his much-anticipated book *Man in the Music* will be released on November 1st, and now he's just about to release a print version of his eBook, *Earth Song.* Thank you for joining us, Joe! Here's what I would like to know first. Why did you choose to single out "Earth Song" and write a separate piece on it? Do you have a special affinity for the song yourself, or did you simply become intrigued by

Michael's process – or obsession – with the song as you were researching for *Man in the Music?*

Joe: I've always loved "Earth Song." The power and majesty and passion of the song always just struck a deep chord with me. When I was working on *Man in the Music*, though, I was listening to all of Michael's work so closely that many songs made new impressions. "Earth Song" was one of them. The more I learned about it and the more I listened, the more convinced I became that this was Michael's most important song. It encompassed so much. The call and response with the choir, to me, is one of the most powerful moments in the history of music. Yet there was so little recognition for the song among critics. Very little had been written about it that wasn't condescending and dismissive. So I wanted to somehow write about it in a way that would communicate its power – and I was excited about the prospect of really being able to zoom in on one song and do all the interviews and research with that kind of focus and depth.

Willa: I loved that! The level of detail you provide is wonderful, and I love the way your book provides insights both into "Earth Song" and into Michael Jackson's creative process as well. You begin your book by discussing how our world is in peril, and with descriptions of him experiencing that peril as an almost physical, wordless pain – and then you show him beginning to channel and shape and express those profound feelings into music. Can you tell us more about this process, and some key moments for how "Earth Song" came to be what we experience today?

Joe: Sure. I think, first of all, the process of "Earth Song" provides a great window into how Michael operated as an artist. That's what made it so much fun to write. You start making connections, putting pieces together. For example, I spoke with Matt Forger about this original concept of "Earth Song" as a trilogy (with an orchestral part, the song, and a spoken poem); after learning that, I returned to Bill Bottrell to figure out who the composer was that Michael was collaborating with and what it sounded like; Bill led me to Jorge del Barrio, who I subsequently learned worked with Michael on songs like "Who Is It" and "Morphine" as well. Through del Barrio I learned some wonderful insights about the concept and feel Michael was aiming for and how it transformed. So you speak to different people and all kinds of new connections emerge: new details, new angles. And you learn how carefully and thoughtfully Michael went about his work. In interviews, Michael tended to be really vague about his creative process, but what "Earth Song" reveals is how obsessed he was with every detail of his work from inception all the way to the final mix. He surrounded himself with great talent, but it was his creative vision and perfectionism that drove his projects.

Willa: You just highlighted something that really struck me when reading your book. You show that he was very knowledgeable and involved in the actual mechanics of creating "Earth Song" – that he was involved in every stage of the process. But in inter-views he did tend to be vague about that, as you say, and kind of distanced himself from that aspect somewhat, focusing more on inspiration and being receptive to the song itself. He said in a number of interviews that the music just came to him and "fell in his lap." You write in your book that he often told himself to "Let the music create itself," and you tie this back to a quotation from John Lennon that he kept on display as a reminder to himself while working on "Earth Song":

> "When the real music comes to me," it read, "the music of the spheres, the music that surpasseth understanding – that has nothing to do with me, 'cause I'm just the channel. The only joy for me is for it to be given to me, and to transcribe it like a medium…. Those moments are what I live for.

When I read this section of your book, I immediately thought of the Romantics. If we look at drafts of their poems, they did revise them and were in fact very knowledgeable and involved in the craft of creating poetry. They were skilled wordsmiths. But like Michael Jackson, they were reluctant to talk about that. They preferred to talk about creating poetry as an act of inspiration rather than craftsmanship, and tended to say they were merely scribes – writing down the words that some creative impulse larger than themselves expressed through them – rather than creators, which is an idea Michael Jackson frequently expressed. In fact, he kind of struggled to explain that during his deposition for the 1994 plagiarism case for "Dangerous," saying that he did write all of his songs, but in a way he didn't – they just came to him. I know you've studied the Romantics, so you know a lot more about this than I do. I was wondering if you could talk a bit about this Romantic ideal of the artist as merely a receptive channel for creativity to flow through, rather than a creator, and how that's reflected two centuries later in John Lennon and Michael Jackson.

Joe: A common metaphor in Romantic poetry is the Aeolian harp: When the wind blows, the music comes. You don't force it. You wait for it.

Willa: That's beautiful.

Joe: Michael believed strongly in that principle. But that being said, Michael was without question a craftsman. He rarely released work in raw form. Another metaphor he liked to use to illustrate his creative process is Michelangelo's philosophy that inside every piece of marble or stone is a "sleeping form." His job as an artist, then, was to chip away, sculpt, polish, until he "freed" what was latent. So it requires a great deal of work. You might have a vision of what it should look like, but you have to be in tune through-out the process and you have to work hard to realize it.

Willa: What a wonderful image! I love that idea of the "sleeping form," and it really clarifies how creativity requires both inspiration and craftsmanship. The idea of the song reveals itself to you and creates itself, as Michael Jackson liked to say, yet it requires the skill and dedication of a craftsman to free it.

Joie: Joe, in your book you talk about the absurdity of the fact that "Earth Song" was never released as a single in the U.S. even though Michael's previous U.S. single, "You Are Not Alone," debuted at number one. And yet, in other parts of the world, "Earth Song" was not only released as a single but went to number one in 15 countries. I agree with you when you say that decision was pretty telling – that the 'powers that be' didn't feel the land of excess would tolerate a song with such an 'in-your-face' look at the human condition. But, I believe that decision was a huge mistake. I think, had it been released here, it would have done very well. Despite the dismissive reviews it received, it is a difficult song to ignore and I think it would have gotten significant radio play if it had been offered to the stations.

Joe: You could be right. It's hard to know. On the one hand, Michael's popularity had waned in the U.S. because of the 1993 allegations. But his first two singles reached the Top 5. It's odd how quickly Sony seemed to bail on the album after that in terms of singles. It would have been nice to at least see the song given a chance with American audiences.

Joie: I love the way you compared "Earth Song" to John Lennon's "Imagine," saying that they both ask the listener to care for the world we have rather than dreaming of an afterlife. But can you talk a little bit about your statement that "Imagine" is more palatable to the average music listener than "Earth Song"?

Joe: Well, "Imagine" is an absolutely beautiful song that also happens to be quite subversive. Because it is so pleasant to listen to, and evokes such nostalgia, however, many people don't really catch on to the latter part. It calls for revolution, but plays amicably in dentist's offices and department stores. So some of its impact can be blunted in that way. When it plays at Times Square on New Year's Eve, it serves as a kind of feel-good anthem. There is nothing wrong with that. In fact, I think "Heal the World" is similar in terms of tone and psychological effect. But "Earth Song" is different. It has a different urgency and intensity to it. Imagine "Earth Song" blaring out of the speakers at full blast on New Year's. Better yet, imagine Michael performing it. Audiences would probably be stunned. The song wasn't designed to make people feel good; it was designed to prick people's consciences, to wake people up.

Joie: Which only makes me wonder all the more how it might have been received had it been given proper promotion and radio play in the U.S.

Willa: And if it didn't do well here, that would say something important too, since it did do well in many other countries.

Joe: Great, prophetic art is often neglected or misunderstood in its time. There are so many examples of this, from Blake to Van Gogh to Mozart to Picasso. Michael was a student of history and art and he understood this. He was confident that the work he created would hold up over time. "Earth Song" is a song that was, and continues to be, massively popular throughout the world. But ultimately it was a song that was going against the grain — so the resistance, from corporate executives, critics and other gatekeepers, makes sense.

"I respect the secrets and magic of nature. That's why it makes me so angry when I see these things that are happening in our world—I really, truly worry. Every second, I hear, the size of a football field is torn down in the Amazon. I mean, that kind of stuff really bothers me. That's why I write these kinds of songs, you know, to give some sense of awareness and awakening and hope to people. I love the planet. I love trees. I have this thing for trees—and the colors and the changing of leaves. *I love it!* And I respect those kinds of things. I really feel that nature is trying so hard to compensate for man's mismanagement of the planet. The planet is sick, like a fever. If we don't fix it now, it's at the point of no return. This is our last chance to fix this problem that we have. It's like a runaway train. And the time has come. *This is it.* People are always saying, 'Oh, *they'll* take care of it, the government will do it.' *They*? *They* who? It starts with us. It's *us*! Or it will never be done."

—Michael Jackson, June 2009

ABOUT THE AUTHOR

JOSEPH VOGEL is the author of five books, including *Man in the Music: The Creative Life and Work of Michael Jackson* and *The Obama Movement*. He writes for *The Atlantic* and *The Huffington Post* and resides in Rochester, New York.

3181623R10065

Printed in Great Britain
by Amazon.co.uk, Ltd.,
Marston Gate.